CHRISTOPHER DRESSER
TEXTILES

Harry Lyons

CHRISTOPHER DRESSER
TEXTILES

ACC Art Books

© 2018 Harry Lyons
World copyright reserved

ISBN: 978 185149 882 6

The right of Harry Lyons to be identified as the author of this work has been asserted by him in accordance with the Copyright, Designs and Patents Act 1988

All rights reserved. No part of this publication may be reproduced, stored in a retrieval system, or transmitted in any form or by any means electronic, mechanical, photocopying, recording or otherwise, without the prior permission of the publisher.

The author and publisher gratefully acknowledge the permission granted to reproduce the copyright material in this book. Every effort has been made to trace copyright holders and to obtain their permission for the use of copyright material. Any errors or omissions are entirely unintentional and should be addressed to the publisher.

British Library Cataloguing-in-Publication Data
A catalogue record for this book is available from the British Library

Many of the images in this book are reproduced from archive sources 'as is' and cannot be removed, cleaned, etc. for conservation reasons.

Printed in China
for ACC Art Books Ltd, Woodbridge, Suffolk, IP12 4SD, UK

www.accartbooks.com

CONTENTS

Introduction	6
The First Designer for Industry	10
The Aesthetic Movement	32
Abstraction	34
Textile Design	38
Manufacturers	46
Index	127

Introduction

Christopher Dresser variously described himself as a 'botanist', 'artist', 'architect', 'ornamentist' and a 'designer'. As a botanist, he was appointed to teach Botany as Applied to Art at the South Kensington School of Design in 1855. His achievements in botany, both as an art teacher and as a botanist per se, gained international recognition in 1860 when Jena University conferred on him a doctorate for a paper on plant morphology and three books that he wrote on botany. However, it is as a designer that Dresser will be remembered. In the new industrial world of the nineteenth century, Dresser was the first designer to understand that machinery was a good servant but a poor master and with this end in mind he made it his business to understand how machines worked. This understanding allowed Dresser to translate his designs deftly into a configuration that could be manufactured without further adaptation—a criticism voiced by manufacturers against the new generation of designers. It was his success in producing designs ready for execution that gained him credibility and respect from manufacturers, which in turn gave him the largest design practice in Britain by 1870. Equally, it was his success in promoting design at affordable prices that attracted his popular following in the press. Dresser was the first Victorian to address, in any sustained manner, the domestic decorative needs of the whole population. The Design Reform movement of the 1840s was the brainchild of 'gentlemen' under the patronage of HRH Prince Albert, a group which having pointed the way for others to follow had no ambition to keep designing on their own account. George Wallis, his headmaster at the School of Design, and Owen Jones, Dresser's mentor,[1] were exceptions in this group and it was Jones who championed 'The People's Palaces' at Sydenham and

Alexandra Park; a project and a philosophy with which Dresser was associated from an early stage. It was Wallis who criticised the practice of contemporary art education, which taught down from the pinnacle of the so-called fine arts instead of firstly accustoming the population to the enjoyment of well-designed objects of everyday life and then leading them up to the appreciation of painting and sculpture. In addition to being an advocate of design reform and its application of art principles to manufacturing, Dresser was also a competent and innovative practitioner of the arts and crafts—witness his designs for Linthorpe and Ault in ceramics and Clutha glass for James Couper, Glasgow—and that takes no account of the oriental arts and crafts which Dresser selected for wholesale import into the UK through the importing companies he advised. As I argue later in the book, Dresser's contribution to the Aesthetic movement was on both an intellectual and a practical level. By importing and ensuring a plentiful supply of affordable *objets*, the Aesthetic movement had a firm foundation on which people could participate and feel involved. I first learned about Dr Christopher Dresser in the 1980s, and ten years later I was fortunate to have an antiques shop from which I could pursue my interest in Dresser's designs. It was a time when the mention of Christopher Dresser was likely to attract the response, 'Christopher Who?' Those who recognised the name had usually seen Dresser's pre-modernist designs in silver-plate and were surprised to learn of his design work in other areas. This led to the question in the 1990s: 'Why does the name "William Morris" attract higher recognition than "Christopher Dresser"?' In reality, the name of Dresser was more widely known in 1880 than that of his contemporary, William Morris (1834–1896).[2] There are several reasons. Firstly, Dresser, through ill health and financial stress in the 1880s, abruptly withdrew from his public 'mission' of design reform to raise the standards of British 'good taste'. He restricted his activity—albeit with notable exceptions—to directing his studio and promoting sales of textiles, wallpaper and floor coverings using flat two-dimensional ornament. As a result, Dresser's name was not placed before the public in the same way as before. An obituary in 1904 noted that: '*At one time, the sudden death of Dr Dresser... would have caused a larger amount of regret than at present...His name, however, will be recalled if ever anyone should have the courage to write a history of ornament since 1851.*'[3] Secondly, Morris had a shop on Oxford Street, London for some 50 years selling the Morris brand. In comparison, Dresser's retail efforts through the Art Furnishers' Alliance, Bond Street lasted only three years before closing in May 1883. Thirdly, the Morris brand, by virtue of its cost through being labour-intensive, sold to the expensive end of the market and thereby attracted a certain cachet. Fourthly, the Morris brand relied on traditional established designs and colourings in line with what the upper echelons of society were familiar with from birth. It was from this same class that British art historians in the twentieth century were to be found. Clisby Kemp, himself an art historian, writing in *The Modern Interior* in 1964 claimed that: '*...Morris was a medievalist, a sentimentalist, and an outrageous romantic, and, because upper middle class liberals in Britain are possessed of these qualities in abundance, they have taken Morris to their hearts and made him a hero. And because most of our historians of economic, social and aesthetic change, came, until comparatively recently from that same class, Morris has been credited with many achievements for which he was not wholly* *responsible...'*[4] Not much changed between Kemp's article in 1964 and the 1990s, when the first two books on Dresser were published.[5] These were followed by three international exhibitions of his work: in Milan, 2001 for the Triennale; at Koriyama, Japan in 2002; and shortly after, in 2004, a shared exhibition between Cooper Hewitt, Smithsonian Design Museum, New York and the V&A, London on the centenary of Dresser's death.[6] It has to be noticed that at Milan, New York and London, these important exhibitions were curated by a dealer in the trade, Michael Whiteway, and the items exhibited were largely provided by British and American collectors and dealers. It is also notable that scholarship in Dresser studies has been led and supported, with notable exceptions, by those outside the museum world. From the early 1880s, the story of Dresser's life and achievements was recorded and secured for future generations due to two important interventions. Firstly, Charles Holme, as editor of *The Studio* magazine, interviewed and wrote on Dresser in 1898 and secondly, Nikolaus Pevsner, in 1936, who wrote an article in the context of Modernism, for the *Architectural Review*[7] after visiting Dresser's daughter, Ada Dresser. After World War Two, the important Exhibition of Victorian and Edwardian Decorative Arts in 1952,[8] identified, and led the way to saving, much of the best of the remaining Victorian decorative arts—at a time when Victorian design was unpopular and perceived as gloomy. As Peter Floud, the then Curator of the Circulation Department, said in a BBC broadcast, *'if we do not record the work of the Victorians before the last survivors disappear, we will lose it; as the generations pass, families that possess "gems" from the Victorian age will not know of their significance.'*[9] Following the rediscovery of Dresser's work in 1952, the momentum of the work that led to it was not maintained. Consequently, many opportunities were lost to record first-hand memories from those active in British design in Victorian times.[10] Fortunately, in 1968 Stuart Durant, the art historian, interviewed the last survivor of the Dresser Studio, Frederick Burrows. Burrows, then 90 years old, was still able to impart valuable first-hand memories of working with Dresser. Interest was maintained by an important exhibition held in 1971 by two dealers,[11] encouraged and facilitated through the offices of Andrew McIntosh Patrick of the Fine Art Society. In 1979, an exhibition curated by Michael Collins was held at the Camden Arts Centre, which later travelled to Middlesbrough[12] and Cologne, thereby introducing Dresser to a new constituency in Germany. Enthusiasm for Dresser in continental Europe was reinforced by an exhibition at Hereford Museum, 2007, which travelled on to Ghent, Prague and Herford, Germany. Throughout the post-war period there were loyal collectors and supporters, such as Charles Handley-Read and John Scott, always on hand to encourage and support research, recognising that there was still more to discover on Dresser. Each new discovery and exhibition on Dresser triggers recognition and discovery on a wider and yet wider circle. One such exhibition was *Into Africa* 2007, held by the Dorman Museum, featuring Dresser's textile designs for West Africa.[13] The resulting publicity spurred one reader to contact the museum with information and examples of work by her great-grandfather, Leo Cheyne, an apprentice to Dresser in 1878. It is possible that it needed a century or more of research and contemplation to put Dresser into context and to understand the Dresser brand. Dresser had a structured argument and he had thought his ideas through. He was particularly sensitive to the new aspiring middle class, often the first generation in their family to have the money with which to furnish and improve their domestic surrounds—but needing 'guidance'. For example, he was always careful to design for customers across the social spectrum; the rich as well as the poor. He walked a fine line between giving helpful advice and being patronising. He understood the aspiration to buy 'the best' and the confusion of customers which resulted from a bewildering array of furnishings in the shops with poorly trained shop staff.[14] For a new generation, perhaps unaccustomed to gracious living, he was wise to promote his designs in room settings. Dresser knew how to use the power of the press and he travelled the country giving lectures, which were duly reported. The 'missionary' zeal with which Dresser marketed his ideas was received better in Europe, the USA and Japan than a more formal Britain. Dresser had passion and, as the New York Times affectionately remarked: 'he could talk one to the death';[15] perhaps not an image with which many of his British peers would have felt comfortable. Dresser was a Victorian but that did not prevent him being 'modern' and, above all, innovative.[16] Writing in Japan, Dresser declared: *'Nothing can be more stupid than our pig-headed persistence in old methods. Progress is no longer possible if we only do what our forefathers did; and the gulf which separates one manufacture from another must be crossed if we are to advance as we should.'*[17] In the words of a former staff assistant, Frederick Burrows: *'He never permitted technical limitations to inhibit his designing.'* There were many notable Victorian artists who excelled in the decorative arts in the 1860s, such as Burges and Godwin, both of whom shared Dresser's enthusiasm for Japan, but Dresser stood out by shouldering the burden of design reform, together with his concern for inclusion of all levels of society. He thereby laid a larger, more secure, foundation on which Modernism in the twentieth century was to develop and flourish. The rising generation of the 1870s and 1880s, growing up with Dresser, were to become the style gurus, designers and customers of the early twentieth century and were conditioned for whatever the Bauhaus and Modernism might bring.

1. 'Jones Made Me Think'. A memorial lecture for Jones given by Dresser at the South Kensington Museum. *The Architect*, 26 September 1874.
2. The British Library's electronic search engine for British newspapers gives more mentions of 'Dr Dresser' than 'William Morris' in the period 1870–1880, once the search references to others sharing the name 'Dr Dresser' and 'William Morris' are deleted.
3. *Architect and Contract Reporter*, Vol.LXXII, 1904, p.360.
4. Harling, Robert and Kemp, Clisby (1964) *The Modern Interior. House & Garden*. New York, p.14.
5. Halén, Widar (1990) *Christopher Dresser*. Phaidon, London. Durant, Stuart (1993) *Christopher Dresser*. Ernst & Sohn, London.
6. In 1997, I wrote to the Director of the V&A proposing that an exhibition of Dresser's work should be planned for 2004—having been advised that the time frame in which to mount an exhibition was seven years. I duly received a reply that I was the first to suggest such an exhibition.
7. *Architectural Review*, 1937, pp.183–6.
8. Mounted by the V&A to commemorate the centenary of the Great Exhibition.
9. *The Listener*, 11 September 1952.
10. Cecil Tattersall, Dresser's chief designer from 1894 to 1904, wrote to the V&A, following the Exhibition of Victorian and Edwardian Decorative Arts, observing that his offer to help had not been taken up.
11. Richard Dennis and John Jesse.
12. Jonathan Le Vine, Curator of the Dorman Museum, facilitated the Middlesbrough exhibition.
13. Curated by Ken Sedman, Dorman Museum.
14. 'Hindrances to the Progress of Applied Art'. *Journal of the Society of Arts*, 1872, pp.435–443, and subsequent readers' letters.
15. *New York Times*, 6 May 1877.
16. 'Modern and innovative' in the sense that both Marlborough and Wellington were 'modern and innovative' military commanders—unlike Field Marshal Haig and Admiral Jellicoe, neither of whom was 'modern and innovative' in their conduct during World War One.
17. Dresser, Christopher (1994) *Traditional Arts and Crafts of Japan*. Dover Publications, New York, p.446.

Christopher Dresser from a carte de visite, c.1860. (Courtesy of the Linnean Society)

The First Designer for Industry

In 1851, two 16 year olds, William Morris and Christopher Dresser, separately visited the Great Exhibition of the Works of All Nations, in the newly constructed Crystal Palace in Hyde Park, London. Morris, who was in the company of his family, was reluctant to enter, according to some reports. It is easy to imagine that Dresser was filled with enthusiasm and curiosity as a student at the School of Design. This massive exhibition was a popular and financial success, and it clearly showed off Britain's dominance in the industrial sphere. However, there was widespread realisation that the designs of British goods produced with the nation's magnificent machines were conspicuously inferior to the designs of goods produced by other nations, particularly France. The British Government recognised this as a national failure, which it attempted to redress throughout the next decade by expanding the teaching of applied art and increasing the number of art schools. Morris and Dresser would have agreed that the Great Exhibition failed in design terms, but the two contemporaries had very different thoughts on the cause of the failure. Morris, who in time became the soul of the arts and crafts movement, ascribed the blame for Britain's lack of success in the realm of design to its abandonment of the principles of the medieval guilds. He argued that these principles, whereby artist-craftsmen could oversee all stages of production of the objects they created, instilled pride in one's work and led to good design. In contrast, Dresser came to believe that, because the Industrial Revolution was there to stay, the solution to the problem of consistently producing good design lay in an understanding of machines and how they worked. In the new machine age of mass production, industrial processes were necessarily divided into separate stages of production. For example, in ceramics, different workers prepared clay, made moulds, formed wares, applied decoration, prepared glazes, and fired the kilns. The industrial process was a team effort. Because successful mass production required disciplined teamwork, taking pride in one's work was a matter for the team as much as it was for one's own individual skills and abilities. In Britain in the 1850s, it was common practice to recruit pattern drawers, as they were known, from the existing workforce, usually without any formal art training. Because they lacked training in artistic principles and their application to the manufacturing process, their work was typically conservative and did not contribute to the production of goods with high levels of artistic quality and originality. Due to steps taken by the Department of Science and Art to improve educational facilities, opportunities and training a great deal of progress was made. Indeed, the positive results of this policy were readily apparent in the greatly improved quality of the British displays at the London International Exhibition, 1862.

A Mission to Improve British Taste

Christopher Dresser, born in Glasgow on 4 July 1834, was the second son of a Customs and Excise officer, from a family who had provided several generations of tax collectors to the Inland Revenue. When he was four, Dresser's family moved to London, and subsequently to Bandon, Co. Cork, where Dresser

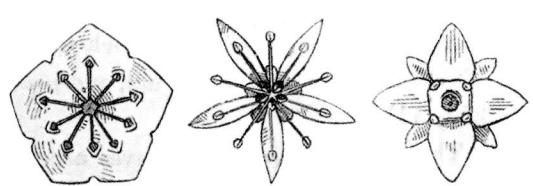

Diagrammatical representation of the nightshade flower (left), the lily (centre) and alchemilla (right). *Unity in Variety*, page 83.

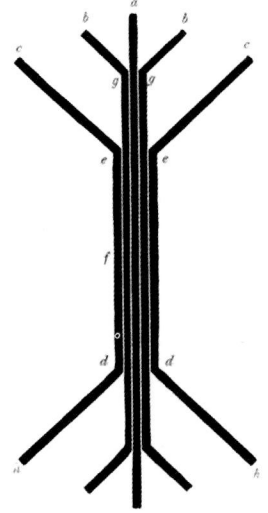

A diagram representing the stem and branches of a plant above ground reflecting the root system below ground. Diagram from Dresser's *Unity in Variety*, page 27.

received what he claimed to be his basic education. Dresser had fond memories of his time in Co. Cork for later, when writing on Japan, he was to recall the colourings of the Cork coastline. Dresser also mentioned a family rebuke over his swap of a small box, gifted by his father, for a box of water-colours.[1] Water-colours were a medium which he used throughout his life and examples of this can be seen today in the surviving records of the Minton and the Royal Worcester archives. The Dresser family moved to London in the mid-1840s, where Dresser père was posted to the Revenue's headquarters. In 1847, the young Christopher, aged 13, gained a place at the School of Design at Somerset House. It is in the School of Design that Dresser learned about conventional treatment of objects. Dresser was a conscientious student but not wholly uncritical of the school; often referring to the fact that of the lecturers who taught him in Art Applied to Industry, only one, in ceramics, had any practical experience of the workshop, and moreover, he doubted that his lecturer in textiles had seen a yard of calico printed in his life.[2]

Dresser was well regarded at the School of Design and on the conclusion of his studies, he was appointed to teach Botany as Applied to Art to the female School of Design. Dresser was, if anything, practical and he grasped the study of botany wholeheartedly, not only in its application to art but also as a science. He attended chemistry lectures so as to comprehend the growth and structure of plants. He applied himself to this field and within five years he was to become the author of three books on botany,[3] all of which were intended to facilitate understanding and simplify the subject for readers. In *The Popular Manual of Botany*, described as a 'ladies' book', he avoided Latin names, preferring to use the vernacular. His books went to reprints. The sketches accompanying these books were an early manifestation of Dresser's imagery in his later designs for textiles and ceramics. Dresser provided an illustrative plate, XCVII, for Owen Jones' *Grammar of Ornament* published in 1856. He wrote a series of articles for the *Art Journal* in 1857 in which he discussed how an artist should view plants and trees—trees should be viewed from the side and plants and flowers from above; important in relation to the manufacture of carpets where a good design should give the feeling of walking on a meadow. The unnatural depiction of trees or lakes to be walked over was an issue for Dresser. It is also of interest that as an adjunct to his writings, Dresser was granted a patent for his method of 'nature printing' of the leaf.[4]

An event that occurred in 1860 profoundly validated Dresser's work in botany. On the strength of his three books and an academic paper he wrote on plant morphology, he was awarded a doctorate from Jena University in Germany. At that time, under the direction of Professor Schleiden, Jena University was regarded as one of the world's most progressive centres for botany studies. Dr Dresser was proud of his award, never having attended university himself,

Owen Jones (1809–1874), architect and designer, and author of *Grammar of Ornament*. Dresser worked with Jones between 1855 and c.1865.

and he was to use the title on every possible occasion, probably to balance his lack of formal academic qualifications. In 1859, as Dresser was developing his career in botany, he was approached by manufacturers wanting designs to use in their displays at the forthcoming London International Exhibition (1862), then being planned. Writing in 1862 in the trade magazine *The Builder*, Dresser mentioned: '… *at special request I [Dresser] furnished many designs to…manufacturers to be wrought for the [1862 Exhibition]—perhaps as many as any individual: yet, [I] had to meet the requirements of an active scientific life…*' Manufacturers in the decorative arts were responding to government encouragement to approach the schools of design for advice and ideas on how to improve on their modest performance in the decorative arts at the 1851 exhibition. Floral forms were predominant in the decorative arts at this time. Following on from Pugin's *Floriated Ornament*, Dresser was well positioned to assist through teaching Botany as Applied to Art in the School of Art and Design in South Kensington. Consequently, the period 1859–1862 was a very intensive and busy time for Dresser with his teaching responsibilities, bringing three books on botany to publication, and in his new role of consultant to manufacturers. The *Art Journal* critic was, in general, supportive but he owned to finding the book 'startling' because of the newness of the designs, although he admitted to admiring some wallpapers designed on Dresser's principles. The *Art Journal* report indicates that Dresser was creating a style of his own—something that was later confirmed in an article by Caspar Purdon Clarke.[5] Clarke, reflecting on this period, referred to Dresser's designs as a distinct 'new English' style.[6] By virtue of his rare combination of professional assets, which included training in design and a lectureship in botany at the South Kensington School of Design, Dresser became a sought-after design consultant to manufacturers. He referred to this period, which commenced in 1859, as his first opportunity to earn money for his designs. He executed designs for international companies, such as Minton and Wedgwood.

Other companies trading internationally would have included Coalbrookdale, in metalwork, and several textile and wallpaper manufacturers. The International Exhibition (1862) was one of two watershed moments in Dresser's career.[7] Dresser found that he could make a positive future for himself and his family from his ability to design for the decorative arts. He comes across in 1862 as someone who has found himself and who is comfortable in his new chosen profession as an artist-designer. Dresser was to write some nine years later: *'That I was intended by nature as an artist I doubt not.'*[8] Interestingly, Dresser's account of the 1862 Exhibition contains the only comment by Dresser on the work of Morris, Marshall, Faulkner & Co., in which William Morris was a co-founder. Dresser remarked on some gilded drawing-room chairs constructed with a seat extended to the rear to provide a base for strengthening the uprights: *'...we cannot commend them as works of beauty... (If the construction principle were) modified and incorporated with elegance of form, an advance would be achieved...'*

Dresser's growing confidence allowed him to challenge some of the received wisdom on the nature and philosophy of art, particularly John Ruskin's pronouncements on the decorative arts. He referred to Ruskin, perhaps the most revered figure in the art world at that time, as the 'representative of the Natural School'—a riposte to Ruskin's reference to 'the steam whistle party'. Ruskin declared, *'Who would decorate a wall, if he could hang a picture on it?'* In *The Art of Decorative Design* Dresser made the robust response, *'Who would put a picture on the wall, if he could decorate it?'* Dresser followed up with a ringing critique of Ruskin's misunderstanding of the nature of ornamental art. To the ornamental artist, the Alhambra Palace in Granada is superior to the Vatican: *'...(In the Vatican) the general effect seems sacrificed to the exceeding power of the pictorial works: but while the representative of the Natural School seems to have a true feeling for pictorial art, he has little feeling for ornament...for if we take away the elegance of his pen...we have little practical information afforded*

A · MOONLIGHT · SCENE ·

THE · ORIGINAL · ETHIOPIAN · SERENADERS ·

The formal treatment of cats with collar and tie never fails to amuse. Border for vase, jug, etc. Artwork in the Minton archive, c.1867. (Courtesy of Royal Doulton)

Artwork for borders on vases or tiles used for dados. Minton, c.1870. (Courtesy of Royal Doulton)

respecting ornament…' In Dresser's opinion, ornamentation grew out of architecture, but who thinks of architecture when thinking of the Sistine Chapel? The doctrine of Ruskin, Dresser thought, led on to the promotion of naturalistic ornament, which actually perverted the teachings of Nature, and this in turn led on to lakes and trees being pictured on carpets for us to walk over—the very opposite of a 'rosy bed or meadow'. Dresser also revealed that Ruskin had consulted Dresser's books on botany to obtain details of his writings, but Ruskin had not appreciated that these were technical works to be read in the overall context of 'Mother Nature'.[9]

Dresser used his experience of designing for industry as the basis for two books on the decorative arts, which were published in 1862: a guide to the 1862 London exhibition, *The Development of Ornamental Art in the International Exhibition*, and a book for students, *The Art of Decorative Design*. These books were educational and written to help readers understand the essence of design. In *The Development of Ornamental Art*, which appeared within a fortnight of the exhibition's opening, Dresser guided readers around the exhibits, commenting on both their strong and weak points. In *The Art of Decorative Design* Dresser delved into the very soul of art, its history and its theory. In order to help students better understand the principles of art, he wrote this book in simple language and analysed and dissected the theory of ornament like a science—remembering his own difficulties as a student in getting to grips with the theory of ornament from the standpoint of his own limited educational background: *'In ornament, as in science, it is necessary to have recourse to an analytical method. The deep insight into the mysteries of the atomic world…is due to the energy displayed in the analysis of substances…'*[10] One chapter in the book was devoted to discussion on the subtlety of the curve, and another on proportion. Dresser championed Owen Jones' principle of making proportions subtle for aesthetic reasons, that is 8:5 and not 4:2. Zeising's 'golden cut' was also examined in this context. One important record of Dresser from this period is a sketchbook, now in Ipswich Museum, showing many pencil drawings and other sketches on pieces of paper and envelopes. Many of these can be identified as work Dresser did for the 1862 exhibition and some as preliminary sketches for the 1867 Paris exhibition, notably for Elkington & Co. in silver-plate, thus dating the notebook to the early 1860s. Dresser explained that the 'scraps' on which he sketched his designs resulted from being, on occasion, subject to an 'influence' in his creation of sketches. Of one occasion in the early 1860s, he wrote: *'…I commenced to draw, when without the least effort of which I was conscious, and without exercising, so far as I know, any control over my pencil, forms and compositions which were new and vigorous, yet often eccentric, were produced with such rapidity, and in such quantities as astonished me. At two o'clock in the morning I had filled many sheets of paper with drawings and feeling fatigue, retired to my chamber. I could not, however, shake off this strange influence: so taking a bundle of letters from my pocket I drew patterns on whatever plain paper they furnished…'*[11] Intriguingly, Dresser thought it necessary to add a footnote to this article declaring that he had not taken any 'unnatural substances'. The decade of the 1860s was to see Dresser gradually reduce his work in botany. In 1868, he gave his last lecture in botany at the School of Design, bringing to a close his teaching career in botany. By the end of the 1860s, Dresser described himself variously as a designer, an artist, an ornamentist and as an architect,[12] and in 1871 Dresser was able to boast that he had by far the largest design practice in Britain. In Victorian times the word 'architect' was used rather loosely and Dresser used the term to describe his work in interior design, for he held no qualifications in the engineering aspects of architecture. *'As an architect, I have as much work as many of my fellows, and as an ornamentist I have much the largest practice in the Kingdom; so far as I know, there is not one branch of art-manufacture that I do not regularly design for, and I hold regular appointments as "art adviser" and chief designer to several of our largest art manufacturing firms'*[13] Following his enhanced reputation subsequent to the International Exhibition, London, 1862, which resulted in numerous press references to his books, and his willingness to give public lectures on botany and art, Dresser embarked on a very personal mission—to raise the standard of good taste in Britain across the social spectrum. Dresser blamed manufacturers for failing to provide the general public with objects of good design at affordable prices. He pointed to an impasse against design progress that stemmed from a combination of manufacturers receiving no overwhelming demand from the public or the shops for better design, and customers perceiving that they could only buy what was available in the shops. In addition to illustrating differences in the quality of the design of goods produced by the participating nations, the Great Exhibition also acquainted British consumers with choices they could make with regard to the goods they purchased. Britain's advancement in the Industrial Revolution produced a new middle class with an increasing disposable income and one that wanted better design. This new class was aware of what else was on offer— not least of all through the international displays which followed the Great Exhibition of the Works of All Nations; an exhibition, which was to set the template for such exhibitions across the world. This aspiration of the nouveau riche was not a problem if you were in the richest top 1–2 per cent of the population. In commissioning a new villa or building an extension, your architect would be available to discuss and locate items and if they were not available, then he would commission them. For the rest of society, including the professional classes, this was not an option; one was limited to what was available in the shops. Dresser sought a solution by offering manufacturers advice on the application of art principles to their products at the cost of an ordinary member of their design staff: *'We understand that Dr. Dresser…is now in Birmingham on a novel and useful mission. At the request of several of our manufacturers, it seems, he has undertaken to pay their works occasional visits, and give them and their workmen the benefits of his talents and experience in the way of suggestions and hints as to their progress and improvement in the application of art to industry. The idea is certainly a new one and there can be little doubt that in practice it will be found highly advantageous…'*[14] Dresser made it his business to understand the industrial process and he had a good knowledge of how machines worked. His detailed knowledge and understanding of the industrial process became a by-word in industry, thus earning the respect of manufacturers. His technical knowledge was such that he was, on occasion, invited to write manuals explaining the industrial process in some of the disciplines in which he worked. His approach to design in industry addressed a common problem with manufacturers who generally found that designers and artists had minimal knowledge of the machines

they designed for and, consequently, their designs were not workable. A year later the *Birmingham Daily Post* was able to report: '...*The Doctor's designs in art-manufactures are in great demand in Birmingham and throughout the country*...'[15] As the *Birmingham Daily Post* points out, what happened in Birmingham happened throughout the country. In other words, his ability to combine the artistic with the practical was highly valued by manufacturers. While Dresser endeavoured to improve design through meeting the needs of manufacturers, he also sought to improve the breadth of knowledge and appreciation of artists and craftsmen. In 1867, Dresser visited the Paris Exhibition, where his designs were exhibited for carpets, textiles, silver, wallpapers and ceramics. He received good notices and several companies for whom he designed were awarded medals. Dresser took full advantage of the opportunity to examine the displays of Europe's top manufacturers and followed this up with a series of articles in a leading art publication of the time, the *Chromolithograph*, discussing the merits of various leading manufacturers, accompanied by illustrations. The articles in the *Chromolithograph* were intended to widen the perspective of the British public, but more importantly these articles were published in a journal hitherto devoted to the fine arts. Dresser was anxious to make the point that the decorative arts ought to be treated as an equal partner to the so-called fine arts; a point he was often to repeat. Dresser believed that the decorative arts required a mental effort not required by the fine arts which, simply put (in the 1860s), was copying the subject matter in front of the artist. Following this in 1870, Dresser began a multi-part series on the principles of design in the *Technical Educator*, a magazine for craftsmen. It was published in parts, over a period of time, in order to make it more affordable. The articles were then assembled and published as a book, *Principles of Decorative Art*, in 1873. This book was followed by another, again in parts, and subsequently in 1876, published as a book, *Studies in Design*. Furthermore, he gave four lectures to the Society of Arts, addressed to an educated audience, which he used to promote his mission to improve good taste in Britain. Dresser next addressed the problem of improving the standards of shops and the advice that they offered to customers. Too often, Dresser thought, this was a question of 'the blind leading the blind'. In a lecture, in 1872, to the Royal Society of Arts, 'Hindrances to the Progress of Applied Art', Dresser created a fictional character, Lady Weakmind, who approached the staff in a store for advice on buying a carpet. The sales assistant directed her to the latest consignment—'just in'—commenting that this consignment was from France. On this advice, Lady Weakmind selected one, thereby giving the sales assistant the opportunity to advise all subsequent customers that this carpet was chosen by Lady Weakmind. Importantly, Dresser also used the occasion of the Alexandra Palace launch to display some of his own wallpaper designs, which carried his name on the selvedge—possibly the first use of a designer label. The use of Dresser's name was intended to give customers a reference point, by claiming that his name on the wallpaper was a

Previous: A furnishing fabric from a company selling extensively in Britain. Cotton roller print. Scheurer Rott, c.1878.

View of Tower Cressy, Notting Hill, London, c.1890, home to Dresser (1869–1883). A substantial house of five storeys plus attic studio and a basement. The 1871 census noted that there were three live-in servants and a cook. The grounds also accommodated the Dresser Studio. The garden was large and extended to the rear of Campden Hill Square, as we know it today.

guarantee that it was manufactured in accordance with art principles. The use of his name on articles was carried through into other products and became a standard part of Dresser's contract with companies that used his services as art advisor. In the case of companies for which he was listed as art advisor, this often meant no more than the article was designed in accordance with art principles—as specifically stated in the prospectus for Linthorpe Art Industries, where the manager, Henry Tooth, was in day-to-day charge and had Dresser's full confidence. Later, from the mid-1880s, coinciding with the downsizing of his house and studio from Notting Hill to Sutton, it is arguable that the use of Dresser's name may have been limited to items he designed personally. Because the use of his name could be subject to abuse, Dresser inserted a clause specifically demanding that his name not be used in connection with any item he had not designed.

Concurrent with his input into Alexandra Palace in 1873, Dresser was also busy arranging the import of oriental items into Britain. These items, by virtue of the 'terms of trade'—or the exchange rates—could be retailed very cheaply and they offered an affordable alternative to the often tawdry articles from the cheap end of the British market. Dresser claimed that many objets of good taste could be imported for one penny at wholesale prices, thus providing a choice of well-designed and crafted items at affordable prices. This project was carried out with Charles, Reynolds & Co., a retailer in the warehousing area of the City of London, to whom Dresser became art advisor. The project soon expanded into a separate wholesale company, Londos, specifically set up to import goods of artistic merit from India, China and Japan. This new importing company also engaged Dresser as its art advisor and in typical Dresser style was launched in May 1876 with good publicity and displays of items in room settings. Following the launch of Londos, Dresser made his plans to visit Philadelphia for the Centennial Exhibition, to be followed by visits to Japan, China and India, where Londos planned to set up bases and engage agents. However, fate intervened in the guise of the Emperor of Japan giving Dresser the freedom to travel wherever he wished in Japan. Dresser took full advantage and spent all of his three months in Japan, leaving some ten days (at the most) to visit China and none in India. On Dresser's return to London in June 1877, he developed four projects to further his aim of improving good taste in Britain—as well as catching up with work in his busy and expanding studio. These were, firstly, the development of Londos as a substantial importing firm from the Orient; secondly, the creation of an 'art industry' complex in Middlesbrough; thirdly, taking on the editorship of the *Furniture Gazette*, perhaps the leading and the most influential weekly magazine for 'the trade'; and finally, the creation of a retail outlet, where staff would provide 'educated advice' to customers. Little is recorded about Londos and its progress in 1877 and afterwards. We know that Dresser sent his son, Christopher, to Japan in December 1877 to work for Londos, but by 1879, Dresser was creating his own importing company together with Charles Holme, an importer from the Indian subcontinent and later the founder of *The Studio* magazine in 1893. It would seem that Dresser believed he could not progress his ideas without more freedom to operate than Londos could contemplate. This new company, Dresser & Holme, opened in June 1879, with wide publicity and a guest list of celebrities in the art world. Goods were arranged in 'room' settings to display the mainly Japanese and Indian goods. As with Londos, Dresser

& Holme was a wholesale operation. As the *Furniture Gazette* reported: '*From the moment we entered, we seemed to have left England and to have been transported to Japan…The establishment is divided into three departments: firstly standard goods, or articles made in large quantities…secondly, goods having a special artistic merit, rarely to be met with… thirdly, a class of goods of ancient manufacture known as curios…[the whole display] is an intellectual treat rarely offered.*'[16] One must marvel at Dresser's care to present Dresser & Holme as an emporium to suit all pockets and all levels of taste. By catering for all and including items to attract the rich as well as those of moderate means, no one might feel patronised. Victorian Britain included many families who were the first generation to have the means to aspire to comfortable living and with the time to appreciate the finer things of life. The professionals and entrepreneurs who formed this class of new money, perhaps without any family tradition of good living, were proud and aspired to the best for themselves and their families. Concurrently, in Middlesbrough, a new art industries complex was taking shape in the then outlying suburb of Linthorpe on the site of a brickworks. Dresser had previously visited Middlesbrough in 1874 and had then suggested to the owner that instead of making bricks, he could use the same clay to make objects of beauty and thus bring more employment into what was then a depressed area. It was intended that the first stage of development would centre on ceramics at the existing site. The new ceramic venture, which was state of the art with gas-controlled kilns, started production in 1879. Work was also completed on a wallpaper factory, in the grounds of the new pottery, and production was started in 1880. However, wallpaper did not survive the year, which may have been due to lack of funding, for in the same year a prospectus seeking investors was published under the title of Linthorpe Art Industries. The prospectus also signalled its intention to produce metalwork and glass. In the event, only the pottery survived the initial launch. Dresser planned to implement his artistic control through the appointment of an artist in whom he had complete confidence— Henry Tooth, with whom he had worked since the early 1870s, using his decorative skills at the Alexandra Palace opening. Linthorpe Pottery was well received, drawing inspiration from many exotic cultures—Japan, China, the Middle East and South America. The pots attracted praise for their novel glazes and shapes, and prices were set in a range to meet all pockets. As reported by a local newspaper, guests at the opening exhibition marvelled at the creation of such beauty made from their 'local muck'. The pottery was launched in London in late 1879, and sales worldwide were co-ordinated by Dresser through Dresser & Holme. Following on from Linthorpe, Dresser's next venture in his mission to educate and improve Britain's taste was to take on a commitment to broaden the art vision of the weekly *Furniture Gazette* by becoming Art Editor. In his first issue (January 1880), which heralded a new format, Dresser produced new graphics and short pieces focusing on particular apects of furniture or furnishings. He consistently reiterated the basic principles of art with illustrations and advice across the spectrum of the decorative arts. It was a brave attempt to reach the core of the furniture and decorative arts trades, where goods were actually produced and he could influence thinking and attitudes. However,

Overleaf: A cotton roller print furnishing fabric, printed by Scheurer Lauth, 1895. (Courtesy of the Dorman Museum. Image by Jason Hynes)

The reception area, Burroughs, Wellcome & Co.'s headquarters, Snow Hill, London, 1885. Dresser was engaged through the Art Furnishers' Alliance. (Courtesy of the Wellcome Foundation)

meeting weekly publishing deadlines was a burden too far and it is not surprising that Dresser withdrew due to illness in December 1880. The same illness led to Dresser formally resigning his position with Linthorpe Art Industries in December 1881. With failing health, Dresser devoted his available energy mainly to the accomplishment of another part of his grand scheme to improve the field of design. He believed that the education and knowledge of shop staff was still a problem in that they were not capable of providing retail customers with 'educated' advice. This led to the creation of a unique retail shop, the Art Furnishers' Alliance, on Bond Street, London, which professed to offer customers advice on interior design and was content to source products not in stock. Dresser was listed as art advisor to the AFA and the shareholder list included many well-known names in the field of the decorative arts, including Arthur Lasenby Liberty. Dresser, himself, had but a single share. The AFA received good publicity and some worthwhile sales, such as the provision of a Moorish scheme of decoration for the main reception area of the headquarters of Burroughs, Wellcome & Co., a pharmaceutical company then establishing itself in new premises in the City of London. However, Dresser found himself confined to bed with a painful illness, as he mentions in his book *Japan*. This coincided with some financial problems, culminating in the Dresser family downsizing from a substantial house in Notting Hill and moving to Sutton, in suburban London.

Little is recorded about the causes for this downturn in Dresser's fortunes, but it is probably safe to assume that he pursued his mission to improve taste in Britain at the expense of both his health and his finances. In 1880, Dresser failed to pay his subscriptions to the Society of Arts and the Linnean Society. In 1882 he also failed to renew his lease on Tower Cressy, thereby suggesting cash-flow problems.

In correspondence following a Society of Arts lecture in 1870, Dresser could boast that he was the most successful designer in Britain with the largest practice, and that there was not a medium in the decorative arts for which he did not design. Dresser had a large personality and his practice needed his presence both in his studio and in making sales. Dresser's absences, in the United States and Japan, and with jury duties at the Paris Exhibition, 1878, may have contributed to his financial problems. Dresser's energy and commanding 'presence' were commented on more than once. In 1877, the *New York Times* affectionately commented: '...*black of beard and bright of eye and who would talk a man into a state which American ingenuity illustrated some time ago by a skeleton in a deal box: but his chat is charming*'.[17] In another first-hand account from a client wallpaper manufacturer in the 1890s: '...*I remember Dresser's visits to the Lightbown factory...between 1893–1899*

Designs for furnishings in the Anglo-Moorish style from the reception hall of Burroughs, Wellcome & Co. at the new headquarters in Snow Hill, London. (Courtesy of the Wellcome Foundation)

to sell designs to my grandfather. That tranquil country house and its smaller private office were always affected as if a small cyclone had visited them. Even the most matter-of-fact ledger clerk was aware that a personality was present: one who could strike the humdrum everyday existence with the elixir of magic.... My grandfather, a small autocrat, enjoyed the change from the conventional routine of buying designs to being told what he must buy and what he could not have... [Dresser had] a Jove-like manner, a voice of authority and an aura.'[18] Dresser's success in selling designs was based on his creativity combined with a commanding presence, and his design practice suffered after 1876, while he addressed other matters. His resulting illness is not surprising and the last straw must have been the burden of meeting weekly deadlines as Art Editor of *The Furniture Gazette*. The reasons for Dresser's move have not been recorded, but one must assume that following family discussions and probably on medical advice, Dresser decided to withdraw from any activity unconnected with his design practice. His new address in Sutton did not have the space for his studio and he rented a terraced house nearby to accommodate it. In conclusion, Dresser saw a faultline in Britain's application of design to 'art-manufactures', which could be confronted with better education. He was passionate about improving design appreciation and set out to improve national awareness. He lectured widely and made the press aware of his activities. He gained an international reputation and was tireless in his pursuit of promoting other cultures. By 1880, Dresser was a household name in Britain and well known in the United States and France. The Aesthetic movement may not have had the initial impetus to flourish in Britain had it not been for Dresser's consistent promotion of Japanese arts and crafts throughout the 1860s and 1870s. Dresser would have been proud to look back on his achievements from the standpoint of the V&A's Victorian and Edwardian Exhibition in 1952. He laid a foundation upon which later movements could build: Macintosh, the Wiener Werksttte and the Bauhaus. The public of 1890 were the younger generation of the 1860s and 1870s, who were growing up when Dresser was a household name and were conditioned to his message. Dresser's simple metalwork in the 1880s, in the form of silverware by James Dixon, Sheffield and the painted galvanised tinware by Richard Perry, Wolverhampton provided strong examples of 'form follows function'. The pure geometry of these pieces was to condition a later public for the appearance of the Bauhaus and Modernism.

The Dresser Studio

Following his move from Notting Hill, London to the commuter suburb of Sutton, Dresser set about restoring his fortunes. In interiors, Dresser was still available to the Art Furnishers' Alliance until its closure in 1883, dealing with decorative schemes such as that commissioned by Burroughs, Wellcome & Co. His contract with James Dixon, Sheffield continued in silverware and his range of domestic silverware set a new high in design; timeless, yet imaginative designs that in the twenty-first century still attract admiration. His imaginative designs for Dixons were matched by the severe, simple geometry of a series of affordable designs for the household, including candlesticks designed for Richard Perry & Sons, Wolverhampton. These candlesticks in galvanised and painted tinware cost upwards of a shilling and attracted an international following, particularly in the United States, where they featured in promotional literature from leading stores. Liberty was the first retail outlet to sell them and they were pictured regularly in the store's catalogues throughout the 1890s. Two more notable achievements from Dresser were Clutha glass, sold exclusively by Liberty in the late 1880s, and ceramics by William Ault in the 1890s, showing Dresser at his most inventive using inspiration from other cultures. Two other commissions he received were for decorations for the Albert Palace in Battersea Park in 1885 and in graphic design he created the front cover for a popular magazine *The Royal Magazine* in December 1899.

However, Dresser's main preoccupation was with the development of his studio. With some ten to twelve staff, whom he selected and trained, the studio output was concerned with textiles, wallpaper and floor coverings from carpets through to linoleum. These were media using flat areas of design and the working up of designs could be safely delegated to his staff and submitted for his approval. The studio would have contained an archive for staff to consult. Dresser maintained strict control of his studio, as evidenced by a former assistant, Frederick Burrows.[19] His assistants were required to present designs in a neat and 'finished' form for presentation to customers. See the example of work presented by Edward Cheyney above, right.

Judging from the registrations of textile designs held by the National Archives for the 1880s, the mainstream of textile design showed little variation from the 1870s though with notable exceptions. These exceptions included two areas in which the hand of Dresser can be seen. There was the appearance of heavy cotton furnishing fabrics, often registered by the former French (then German) textile manufacturers from Alsace to whom Dresser sold designs. One further

A watercolour drawing of work by an apprentice to Dresser, Edward Cheyney, 1878–1883. (Courtesy of the Dorman Museum)

amazing series of designs stands out; the registration of designs for the West African markets in a series believed to depict The Creation. This series is referred to in more depth in the textile section but it is known that the series was created some considerable time before it was produced in 1886 and one can believe in Dresser's personal involvement in these designs. These designs formed the basis of an exhibition in the Dorman Museum, Middlesbrough in 2007. In the mid-1890s a discernible change of style can be detected in the examination of design registrations by textile companies using Dresser as their art advisor, such as F. Steiner & Co. These designs reflected the newer styles of art nouveau, but a glance through the examples illustrated in this book will show a very eclectic mix. This change must have reflected requests from companies selling into a fashionable European market and would have been responded to eagerly by his young and educated staff designers. There was a change of mood generally in the 1890s, not dissimilar to that of the 'swinging sixties', some seventy years later. The arrival of the steam engine had led to an expansion of the customer base for travel. Expansion of the use of electricity and the telephone were becoming commonplace. Figures such as Oscar Wilde and Aubrey Beardsley were prominent in challenging accepted social norms and retail customers among the fashionable world were seasoned travellers, aware of what choices were available throughout Europe, unlike in Dresser's youth. The Aesthetic movement had run its course and customers wanted something new. Dresser's later years saw him increasingly content to travel and attend to sales. However, as claimed by Frederick Burrows, a former staff member who worked in Dresser's studio in 1899, nothing left the studio without Dresser's approval. The rationale of Dresser and his studio in the last decade of his life was to create designs that sold in the market. Dresser was to produce some humourous caricatures for magazines in 1899, including the satirical magazine, *Pick-Me-Up* and a popular publication, *The Royal Magazine*. These reflected his earlier stylised work with 'borders' for Minton.[20]

On 24 November 1904, Dresser was on a sales trip to Mulhouse (then Mühlhausen, Germany) selling his designs in textiles and wallpaper. That evening, in the Central Hotel, he breathed his last due to a heart attack. His office manager, Edwin Jeffreys, and his son, Louis Leo, were despatched from London to take care of the formalities. He was buried in a plot in the Protestant section of the cemetery in Mulhouse. Thirty years later his remains were removed to the town ossiary as the family had not expressed any wishes to maintain the site. Maybe, one day, there will be a suitable memorial in Mulhouse to one who may claim to be the father of design for the decorative arts in an industrial age.

Steinbach-Koechlin. Design for border at the bottom of a curtain. Registered with the British PODR, November 1868.

1. *Journal of the Society of Arts*, 1871, p.352.
2. *Journal of the Society of Arts*, 1871, p.352.
3. *The Rudiments of Botany* (1859); *Unity in Variety* (1859); *The Popular Manual of Botany* (1860).
4. Patent No.2904, 1855.
5. Clarke was a student at the School of Design between 1862 and 1865, when Dresser was a lecturer. Later, Clarke carried out work sourcing good examples of native arts and crafts in Egypt and Persia for Dresser. Clarke later became Director of the South Kensington Museum and the Metropolitan Museum, New York.
6. *Cabinet Maker and Art Furnisher*, July 1892.
7. The second watershed moment was the period 1880–1883, when illness forced Dresser to downsize and relocate to Sutton, which prompted his withdrawal from activities in promoting design reform.
8. *Journal of the Society of Arts*, 1871. See correspondence following Dresser's lecture in 1871.
9. Fourteen years later, James McNeill Whistler was also to cross swords with Ruskin in a celebrated court case. Ruskin, then Slade Professor of Fine Art at Oxford, decried Whistler's *Nocturne in Black and Gold* and its price of 200 guineas as 'Cockney impudence' for 'flinging a pot of paint in the public's face'.
10. *The Art of Decorative Design*.
11. 'On the Production of Ornament under the Influence of Quasi Inspiration', *Warehousemen and Drapers Trade Journal*, 1875.
12. In 1862, Dresser's own description of himself in the Preface to his books reads: 'Professor of Ornamental Art and Botany at the Crystal Palace, Sydenham, Botany Applied to the Fine Arts in the Department of Science and Art, South Kensington Museum, and of Scientific Botany in the Polytechnic Institution, and the London and St Mary's Medical Colleges'.
13. Letter in the *Journal of the Royal Society of Arts*, 1871.
14. *Birmingham Daily Post*, 16 August 1865.
15. *Birmingham Daily Post*, 9 August 1866.
16. *Furniture Gazette*, 21 June 1879.
17. *New York Times*, 6 May 1877.
18. Letter from Alan Sugden to Peter Floud, V&A dated 22 March 1952. See record of the 1952 Victorian and Edwardian Exhibition.
19. Stuart Durant, *Christopher Dresser*, p.41.
20. See illustration on page 15.

The Aesthetic Movement

The Aesthetic movement is not an easy movement to define and means different things to different people. The V&A Exhibition, 2011, gave prominence to the fine arts and the cult of Oscar Wilde over the decorative arts. The Tate Gallery claims in its Glossary of Terms[1] that the Aesthetic movement was a late nineteenth century movement that championed: 'art for art's sake, emphasising the visual and sensual qualities of art and design over practical, moral or narrative considerations'. Dresser would agree neither with the Tate Gallery nor the V&A's take on the Aesthetic movement. Beauty was important but not at the cost of the functional. Unfortunately, there was no organised movement promoting the aesthetic, thus making it difficult to decide who or what to include or exclude. Dresser had a fascination with Japanese crafts. Doubtless, he would have come across Japanese art at the School of Design, but it was the display of Japanese arts and crafts at the London International Exhibition, 1862, curated by the British Ambassador to Japan, Rutherford Alcock, that led to his lifelong interest. Dresser bought many of the articles exhibited by Alcock. He promoted Japanese art at this time, both in his writings[2] and in his lectures to art and literary institutions, notably in Britain's industrial centres. In 1873, together with Sir Edward Lee[3] and Philip Cunliffe-Owen, Dresser arranged for the purchase and transportation of the Japanese village, then on display at the Vienna Exhibition, to the site of Alexandra Palace, together with several craftsmen who would work in the village and sell items to the general public—stamped with a label as a guarantee of authenticity. Dresser was insistent on making well-designed, useful and beautiful objects available to the widest possible selection of society. The Art Furnishers' Alliance (AFA), to which Dresser was art advisor, was a one-stop shop from which to furnish your home, with the

Opposite: Two images of the crowds at the Japanese village, Alexandra Palace.

aim of combining beauty and functionality at all price levels. One notice in the AFA proclaimed the message 'cheap is not ugly'. For twenty years of his life Dresser promoted the arts and crafts of the Middle East and the Orient. He advised and promoted companies that imported crafts of good design in a range to meet all incomes. Dresser made a significant contribution to be considered in any definition of the Aesthetic movement by facilitating a large quantity of affordable items, which allowed for broad public participation. Dresser fully realised that in making objects of good design widely available he was opening a Pandora's box to pale and tawdry imitations; hence his promise to put a stamp of authenticity on goods made in the Japanese village at Alexandra Palace. But it was not only in this practical sphere that Dresser contributed, he promoted Japanese crafts at an intellectual level on the grounds of beauty and in understanding the mindset of the artist and a striving for 'maximum effect with minimum means'.[4] The Aesthetic movement was much more than 'walking down Piccadilly with a lily in your hand'. The idea of a Japanese village with working craftsmen attracted press coverage and public interest and was followed by other similar ventures. In 1885, an Indian village was created by Arthur Liberty for the newly opened Albert Palace, Battersea, with forty-two Indian craftsmen brought in for the occasion.[5] Also in 1885, a Japanese village was created with a complement of Japanese artisans and craftsmen in the middle of Knightsbridge at Humphreys' Hall in the area of today's Trevor Square. The Knightsbridge village attracted much publicity and the D'Oyly Carte Company sent the cast of Gilbert & Sullivan's *The Mikado* there to learn deportment and the use of fans. Dresser was also a good publicist and attracted coverage in both the national and trade press for his ventures. In so doing, he was ensuring that there was a continuing public interest, which together with a constant supply of oriental arts and crafts at affordable prices provided a sound base on which the Aesthetic movement could progress . By so doing, he encouraged a greater number of participants to support the ideas of the 'aesthetic' than could ever have arisen from the cult of Oscar Wilde or the fashionable goings-on in Bedford Park. Look no further than his lectures to the Society of Arts and his book *Japan*, 1882, which went to several reprints.

1. http://www.tate.org.uk/learn/online-resources/glossary/a/aesthetic-movement
2. *Builder and Building News*, 1863.
3. The Commissioner for the Dublin Exhibition, 1865, and a Director of the Alexandra Palace Company.
4. A quote made in the Durant–Burrows interview of 1968 by a former member of Dresser's design team.
5. See *Illustrated London News*, November 1885 for a page of sketches.

Abstraction

Most decorative art is by its nature abstract, presenting three-dimensional objects in a two-dimensional form. Abstract design in the decorative arts, or to use Dresser's terminology, conventional flat design, has been with us since the Bronze Age. However, the 'fine arts', interpreted as painting and sculpture, suggest the twentieth century as a 'start' date for abstract art. The Tate Gallery website proclaims Malevich(1878–1935) and Mondrian (1872–1944) in painting and Naum Gabo (1890–1977) in sculpture as pioneers of abstract art.

However, an examination of textile designs from the late nineteenth century will suggest that two-dimensional abstract art, as well as many other twentieth-century art forms were already in rude health by the year 1900. In three-dimensional art, Dresser's designs in ceramics and glass show three-dimensional abstraction to be equally in rude health.

A brilliant example of Dresser's three-dimensional abstraction is the pot produced by Linthorpe c.1880 and popularly known today as the 'tsunami' vase. The woodblock print *Under the Wave off Kanagawa* by Hokusai was well known in Britain at the time the Linthorpe piece was created and it seems probable that this is the source of Dresser's inspiration. The power of the waves is caught by both Hokusai and Dresser.

Imagine, say, a competition in 1880 to produce an article in ceramics inspired by the Hokusai print. Would anyone expect Minton, Wedgwood and Royal Worcester, for example, to respond with other than a two-dimensional frieze or similar? Dresser responded with a three-dimensional abstracted sculptural design incorporating the spirit and energy of Hokusai's print.

Dresser believed that in contemporary society, the decorative arts were much undervalued and should rate alongside the so-called 'fine' arts. Dresser

'Tsunami' vase.(Courtesy of Michael Whiteway)

Katsushika Hokusai, *Under the Wave off Kanagawa*.

claimed at a lecture given before the Society of Arts in February 1871, that the decorative artist was required to exercise the mind more so than the painter or sculptor who was merely 'copying' his subject matter. Dresser would have absorbed this opinion from his days at the School of Design from 1847. It should be remembered that the School of Design was founded in 1836 to promote the design of decorative art for industry and students of the 'fine' arts were specifically excluded. George Wallis, well known to Dresser as a Keeper at South Kensington Museum, often criticised the practice of teaching down from 'fine' art to the enjoyment of everyday objects. This was the wrong way round. The importance of good design for industry was constantly emphasised and discussed at the School of Design and in the 1850s, after a mediocre British perfomance at the Great Exhibition, the Board of Trade appointed Owen Jones, Richard Redgrave and Dr Lyon Playfair to reorganise art training nationally—three people with whom Dresser would have had regular contact and with whom he worked during the 1850s.

TEXTILES

Textile Design

Dresser worked with textiles all his life and textile design was the largest element of his design practice. He was a pupil of Octavius Hudson at the School of Design and among his achievements at the school was a prize for a floral design based on larkspur in 1853. In the last two decades of his life, the Dresser Studio of some ten to twelve staff provided designs in all areas of two-dimensional, flat decoration for textiles, wallpaper and floor coverings, such as carpets and linoleum. We can deduce that the output from his studio would have been sizeable from the account of Frederick Burrows' time with Dresser.[1] Dresser's chief designer, Cecil Tattersall, claimed that there was not a firm manufacturing wallpapers and cretonnes that Dresser did not do business with,[2] and when the wallpaper combine was formed[3] he frequently travelled to 'Germany'.[4] During his visits to Alsace, Dresser also sold wallpaper designs to Jean Zuber, Rixheim and to the Swiss company, Salubra, Basel.

Fixing a date for the start of Dresser's commercial career in textile design can only be by deduction as there is no record for this; however, it is likely to have been around 1859 when preparations for the 1862 Exhibition were getting under way. In an effort to improve upon Britain's poor showing of ornamental design in 1851, manufacturers were encouraged to approach the Schools of Design for help. It is therefore quite possible that Dresser, then still pursuing his career in botany at the South Kensington School, came into contact with manufacturers who had accepted this challenge—especially so, as floral forms were a staple of textile design at that time.

Records of the 1862 Exhibition show illustrations from the expensive end of the market, and those designers, when credited, were already well known. Dresser, at this stage was establishing his style, and may even have been working with Owen Jones.[5] Nevertheless, it is probable

Previous: Detail of tablecloth by Dresser for John Wilson and manufactured by Ireland Bros, Belfast and Lurgan c.1891. Linen. Double damask. Length 366cm (12 feet), width 122cm (4 feet). Fleur de lys mark of Ireland Bros. (Courtesy of the Dorman Museum. Image by Jason Hynes)

Opposite: For The Creation. A lightweight cotton. Edwards, Cunliffe, Wilson. PODR registered, April 1890.

Dresser's prize-winning textile design, 1853. Printed by Hargreaves for Liddiard & Co. PODR registered, April 1853. Sample in the V&A until 1939. (Courtesy of the National Archives)

that Dresser designed many of the textiles, wallpapers and carpets on display at the 1862 exhibition. These would have included William Fry, Dublin, in poplin and silks, Brinton & Lewis, Kidderminster, in carpets, and Woollams in wallpaper. Thomas Clarkson, Tootal Broadhurst and Lee, and William Fry are all well documented. Textiles from others such as Steinbach Koechlin, Scheurer Lauth and Dollfus-Mieg in Alsace show strong stylistic evidence.[6]

Writing in 1892 in an article reviewing the progress of design in brocades and silks, Caspar Clarke, referred to a significant advance in the 1850s and 1860s.[7] Clarke commented that at this time, design in Britain followed French fashion, except where 'genius intervened'. Such genius, Clarke commented, was to be found in the work of Owen Jones and Dresser. In what appears to be strong support for Dresser, Clarke further commented that Jones' work had the beauty of a snow crystal, whereas Dresser's had warmth.

'...Thus Owen Jones in the fifties tried to free ornament from the restraints imposed by the attempted representation of natural objects. His work was beautiful, but it was the beauty of a snow crystal—wanting in human interest. Then Dr Dresser, who, at first following in the same path, re-admitted natural forms, and was one of the first who showed British manufacturers in many trades that the public would accept and pay good prices for original English designing. But the great change came as a tidal wave; and it would be doing injustice to many if I attempted even to give the leading names of our artist designers of the past twenty years...'[8]

The above account from a contemporary of Dresser's, when applied to textiles generally, suggests that one may identify Dresser designs in the 1860s by looking for a style similar to Jones'. By the 1870s, Dresser had developed his own recognisable style, described in the above quote as 'English' (not mediaeval Early English) style. The term 'English' to describe a new style by Dresser was also used in the description of Crossley carpets by reviewers of the 1871 and 1872 London Exhibitions. Indeed, as the commentator states, his remarks on Dresser's development of an 'English' style were intended to apply 'in many trades' and not just one area of textiles.

The designs of William Fry, Dublin shown at pages 62–64 and the grouping of designs by J.C. Ward, Halifax, as illustrated at pages 104–106, may give an idea of what was in the writer's mind, when he talked

J.W. & C. Ward. Silk and wool, c.1870. (Courtesy of Andrew McIntosh Patrick)

about Dresser's 'new English style'.

After the move from Notting Hill, the workload of the studio would have increased. The emphasis of Dresser's work was in marketing, while his studio produced designs.

There is little doubt that textile design was the most enduring element of Dresser's work and in the latter years, became the staple of his design business.

Surprisingly few identifiable British textile examples remain from the nineteenth century, outside the massive records of the Patent Office Design Registry held at the National Archives. However, records in the PODR give only the name and address of the manufacturer or person who made the registration, and not the designer. By their very nature, most textiles have not survived their brief period of practical use, and those items stored away in a 'bottom drawer' tend to be from the expensive end of the market.

To understand the British textile industry in the nineteenth century, it should be remembered that Britain was manufacturing for sale to a world market. From the very beginning of the Industrial Revolution, Britain absorbed, rehashed and sold designs from every quarter of the globe. A statistic from 1865 neatly makes the point—Britain manufactured in excess of £80 million worth of cotton textiles, of which some £52 million was exported. Britain exported ten times as much as her nearest competitor, France, with a quarter of British exports going to India, and the rest going to all corners of the globe. The companies that supplied this world market included all of the companies that Dresser designed for, and what held good for cotton, could be extended to all branches of textile manufacture. The design influences of this diverse and international market fed back into the native British industry, as can be seen from the range of patterns and styles that Dresser used and which were published in *Modern Ornamentation* (1886).

In the 1870s, Dresser undoubtedly broadened his output in textile design. Indeed, Pevsner noted that Dresser's account books recorded some 158 sketches for silk damasks being sent to Ward in 1869. But what of his work in cotton prints, linen, textured weaves, and woollen goods? This less glamorous end of the market was not recorded, and it can only be assumed that Dresser's work in this area was huge. The PODR records show large numbers of cotton print registrations for sale abroad, such as batiks and turkey reds (including a large number from Steiner), and many of these show themselves to be above the level of mere copies. This may well be where Dresser had a market.

By 1878, Dresser was acting as art advisor to Barlow & Jones, to whom he also sold quilt designs. His connections to Steiner, Stead McAlpin, Swaisland Printing Co., Thomas Clarkson, and Tootal Broadhurst, Lee are all well documented. Textiles from others such as William Fry and Steinbach Koechlin (Mulhouse) provide strong stylistic evidence of a connection.

After 1882, Dresser's work in textiles increased as his involvement with merchant ventures ceased and he re-established his practice after the move from Notting Hill. His work for Liberty in the 1880s would also have facilitated this.

The Dresser Studio designed for flat (two-dimensional) decoration. With two experienced designers, Cecil Tattersall and Edwin Jeffreys, and a group of young artistic apprentices, Dresser could pay attention to stabilising his finances and make sales visits to manufacturers. His studio staff would have been responsible for drawing up and making presentation drawings.[9] Britain was the dominant producer of textiles in a world market and afforded many more sales opportunities for a designer than, say, other areas of Dresser's design practice.

Pevsner, viewing Dresser's account books for the

Steiner cretonne. c.1895. In the style of Voysey. Photograph taken for Pevsner in 1936 from Dresser's archive. No example of this has been identified.

years up to 1885, selected five names as examples of solid, enduring textile companies that Dresser had worked for: Barlow & Jones, Tootal, William Fry, Turnbull & Stockdale, and Liberty. These names are merely representative of those companies still surviving in the twentieth century at the time Pevsner was writing. There were numerous other companies that Dresser worked with, many of which are named in the Manufacturers section (pages 46–112).

Provision of designs was shared amongst Dresser's studio, rebuilt after his move from Notting Hill. There were probably some ten to twelve members in number, which would have included paid assistants and unpaid 'improvers', whose parents paid for their place in the studio, based on Dresser's reputation. Dresser, however, inspected every design that left his studio for suitability for industrial production and for neatness of presentation. According to Burrows, he might say: 'That won't print' and then gently smudge the offending draft with his finger. Those designs that were accepted, he would personally offer to manufacturers.

At some point in the 1890s, Dresser accepted the challenge of designing for a wider selection of styles. Charles Holme, in his article on Dresser specifically referred to a 'later style' and contrasted it with his 'earlier manner', defined by Holme as designs that had appeared in Dresser's own publications. It is thought that this change came in the early 1890s as Voysey, Crane, Morris and Day all established a following amongst industrial manufacturers, not to mention the popular and rival Silver Studio. A practical man, Dresser faced the challenge and the positive identifications of Dresser designs handed down to us by both Holme and Pevsner, show how extensive this was. True to his own precepts of using other styles as a base for inspiration, and adding something of oneself, these designs were not copies. It is unlikely, for example, that Beardsley would have sketched the illustration opposite, nor Voysey that on page 43.

Steiner. Design for printed cotton hanging. PODR registered, February 1899. This design also recorded by Pevsner. Compare the stylisation of the peacocks with the image on page 90. (Courtesy of the National Archives)

Manufacturers

Barlow & Jones, Manchester and Bolton

James Barlow founded his Bolton operation in 1846, following a difficult start in Manchester. He joined with Thomas Jones of Manchester to form Barlow & Jones. In 1875, the company acquired limited liability and shares were offered to, and taken up by, many of the workforce. Barlow & Jones exhibited at London in 1862, Paris in 1867 and 1878 (winning silver), and Chicago in 1893.

Barlow & Jones. Detail of quilt to commemorate the Golden Jubilee of Queen Victoria, 1887, and shown at the Manchester Exhibition, 1887. From a contemporary illustration. A quantity was bought for use at Windsor Castle. This is an interesting example of how Dresser designed for a national occasion.

The Royal Coat of Arms is in the centre above the words 'Victoria Empress', surrounded by seaweed, to symbolise Britain's sea power holding the Empire together. The Prince of Wales' feathers appear in each corner of the field. The Empire of India is represented separately (above the Royal Arms) by the Star of India and the motto 'Heaven's light our guide'. The emblems of the colonies form the innermost border, outside of which is a row of dots and a diamond pattern enclosing concentric circles with stitched lines across to give an op art or spinning effect. This, in turn, is surrounded by a stylised rendering of the English rose, Scottish thistle and the Irish shamrock – representing the three kingdoms; Wales, being a principality, is represented by the Prince of Wales' feathers. There are two further ornamental borders

Barlow & Jones. PODR registrations for quilts, June 1878. Probably exhibited Paris 1878.

Barlow & Jones. Quilt, exhibited at Chicago, 1893. Motifs using stars. Panel reminiscent of 'night' cartoon in *The Art of Decorative Design*. United States eagle treated as the 'winged globe'.

Barlow & Jones. Quilt, exhibited Paris, 1878. (*Art Journal*, 1887)

Ed & Jos Buckley, Manchester

Early history of this company is unknown, though many designs were registered at the PODR between 1890 and 1900.

Opposite: Buckley. Cotton print. PODR registered, November 1897.

Buckley. Cotton print. PODR registered, August 1895.

Thomas Clarkson, Preston and London

By the mid-nineteenth century, Clarkson had developed from its eighteenth-century origins at Bannister Hall, Preston, into a respected national name, well known for the quality of its printing. Clarkson had a London outlet, off Piccadilly Circus, and was described in the Post Office Directory of the time, as 'furniture printers and manufacturers'. Both Dresser and William Morris used the company for printing, as did William Fry, Dublin. Thomas Clarkson was a creditor of the AFA in 1883. In 1893 the company closed and the design archive was bought by Stead McAlpin. The design shown on this page is thought to be in Dresser's handwriting. A forensic expert in handwriting concluded that, *'There was evidence to support the proposition that the pencil annotations had been made by Christopher Dresser'*. Without a forensic examination of the original documents (this was precluded on the grounds of conservation as well as expense), a definitive statement could not be made. Whereas the designs do not all immediately resound as Dresser, there are many stylistic similarities and Dresser could well have been designing to the demands of a specific commission.

T. Clarkson. Working sketch for William Fry, Dublin commission. Instructions read, 'All the leaves are to be (...) those marked are to be cut the same as the others, with dots around the brown and veins inserted' and 'The size of the ground of this part is the best. Please keep it so.'

T. Clarkson. c.1869. Artwork.

Edwards, Cunliffe, Wilson, Glasgow and Manchester

Very little information is known about this company. It was described in the 1887 Post Office Directory for Glasgow as 'Manufacturers for West Africa and commission agents for Algerian markets'. During the 1880s several registrations were made for designs at the PODR. A set of remarkable designs in Dresser's studio was referred to by Frederick Burrows, a former designer in Dresser's studio. These designs were a series of four or five designs '... *depicting the evolution or Creation of the World. These, when manufactured were a complete commercial failure until they began to sell to West Africa...*'[10]

Nikolaus Pevsner, writing in 1937, having inspected the surviving Dresser archive, tended by Dresser's daughter Ada, also confirmed the existence of some

Edwards, Cunliffe, Wilson. Blue, red and yellow 'Easter eggs' with foliage and daises on indigo background. Part of the 'Creation' series for the West African market. Lightweight cotton. PODR No. 61000, 10 November 1886.

Edwards, Cunliffe, Wilson. Red, yellow and blue shields with floral design, interspersed with lightning bolts. Part of the 'Creation' series for the West African market. PODR No. 60998, 10 November 1886.

Edwards, Cunliffe, Wilson. Bright red, yellow and blue three-petal flowers with intertwined 'acorns' on indigo background, part of the 'Creation' series for the West African market. (See *Modern Ornamentation*, plate 5.) PODR No. 60999, 10 November 1886.

designs, illustrating the Days of the Creation '... *something of the genuineness which one must admit and may admire in his earlier work...*'[11]

The search to identify 'The Creation' led me to search the records of the Patent Office Design Registry (PODR) held by the National Archives on the chance that the designs would have been registered. After some ten years searching 750,000 designs in all media, this proved to be the case. Eventually, a provable Dresser design was identified, which had been registered as a cotton print by a West African trading company.[12] This design was entered at the PODR on 10 November 1886 by Edwards, Cunliffe, Wilson along with a further seven designs. The PODR does not reveal which company was commissioned by Edwards, Cunliffe, Wilson to manufacture these lightweight cotton prints but my guess is that this would have been F. Steiner, to whom Dresser was 'art advisor' and who produced a similar design, identified as by Steiner and in the same genre.[13]

Opposite: Edwards, Cunliffe, Wilson. Blue, black, green, white, red and yellow sea urchins on indigo background. Part of the 'Creation' series for the West African market. PODR registered, April 1888.

Edwards, Cunliffe, Wilson. Red, yellow, blue and black oriental-style shields, with intertwining red and yellow striped squiggles on indgo background. Part of the 'Creation' series for the West African market. Cotton print. PODR registered, November 1886.

Edwards, Cunliffe, Wilson. Red, yellow, blue and black 'comets' on indigo background. Part of the 'Creation' series for the West African market. Cotton Print. PODR registered, April 1888.

Sketch from the *Ipswich Sketch Book*, page 54, c.1864. To illustrate *The Comet*. The quote from this poem reads:

> 'Mysterious visitment! Whose beauteous light
> Among the wondering stars so strongly glows
> Like a proud banner in the train of night.'
>
> (Courtesy of Ipswich Museum)

Edwards, Cunliffe, Wilson. Blue, red and yellow stylised sunsets on indigo background. Part of the 'Creation' series for the West African market. PODR registered, November 1886.

Nevertheless, most of the seven designs registered in November 1886 could be regarded as a suitable illustration for The Creation. Further, two of these seven have a striking resemblance to another known Dresser design (see page 54).

An attempt was made to select 'four or five designs' to fit the Creation story, as told in the King James version of the Bible but there were no obvious clues and the unanswered question remained as to why Burrows mentioned 'four or five' designs and not six or seven. The eureka moment came unexpectedly, when a colleague related the story of The Creation according to the beliefs of the Yoruba in West Africa.[14] Observing the cockerel on page 59, my colleague observed that the supreme Yoruba God, Orisha Oludumare, commanded a fellow deity, Olisha Obatala, to descend to the oceans below with an iron chain, a sack of earth and a cockerel. The cockerel was to scatter sand with his toes in order to create land. Oludumare, himself, then descended to create the human race. The process of the Yoruba Creation lasted four days and on the fifth, Oludumare rested.

Of course, Dresser would have made it his business to understand the market he was selling into.

Further designs were registered by Edwards, Cunliffe, Wilson throughout the late 1880s which share the same energy and colour as the 1886 registrations (see, for example, pages 39 and 55). These designs were displayed at an exhibition *Into Africa* at the Dorman Museum.[15]

Edwards, Cunliffe, Wilson. Red, yellow, blue and black cockerels on indigo background. Part of the 'Creation' series for the West African market. PODR registered, November 1886. The cockerel motif appears in *Modern Ornamentation*[16] and was available to the public in 'part' form from December 1885. Nevertheless, it is thought unlikely that a company would have publicly submitted this design to the PODR other than through having title to the design.

William Fry, Dublin

William Fry & Co., Dublin occupied a position in Ireland in the nineteenth century similar to that of Jackson & Graham in London. Fry was both a store and a manufacturer. It employed some forty men in its carpentry workshops, but little is known about its textile manufacturing. The Thomas Clarkson records hold evidence of a manufacturing collaboration with Fry from the 1860s/1870s. Fry was praised for its displays of poplins and silks at the various international exhibitions. At the Dublin Exhibition of 1865, Fry was specifically praised for its encouragement and use of graduates from the Schools of Design.

Dresser's designs for Fry were acknowledged by Mr E. Walsh, the chief designer for Fry, in a statement to the House of Commons Committee enquiring into the State of the Teaching of Art in Ireland, 1869.[17] The most famous and recognisable of Fry's designs is the peacock feather design marketed by Liberty from 1900 as 'Hera'.

'Hera'

The 'Hera' design opposite was registered by William Fry in December 1876. Since 1975 'Hera' has been wrongly identified as a design by the Silver Studio for Liberty & Co., and it featured as such at the Liberty Centennial

Opposite: William Fry. Silk weave. PODR registered, December 1876. (Courtesy of the National Archives. Image by Peter Andow)

Below: Rossendale. Cotton print. Same design as the silk weave opposite. Design registered at PODR, January 1900.

William Fry. Two silk damask designs from the PODR archive, registered June 1866.

Exhibition in 1975. This attribution was in error as the Silver Studio was not established until 1880 and, moreover, there is no reference to this design in the Silver Studio archives.[18] Dresser is the only designer, outside of the company's in-house designer—a Mr E. Walsh—who is identified as designing for Fry & Co.[19] In reply to a House of Commons committee examining the teaching of art in Ireland in 1868, Mr Walsh stated:[20]

'…with regard to the other designers whose designs you used, where did they come from?—We have made one or two designs by Dr. Dresser. I don't recollect that we ever made a design produced by a foreigner; but I may say that at the recent Exhibition in Paris, one of our partners who was there was complimented by the president of a jury…'

It is important to get the background on the origin of this textile correctly stated as the misattribution to the Silver Studio remains uncorrected.[21] The registration of the 'Hera' design was submitted by William Fry, Dublin as a woven silk in December 1876, and twenty-four years later the design was registered by the Rossendale Printing Company, in January 1900, as a cotton print. Dresser is

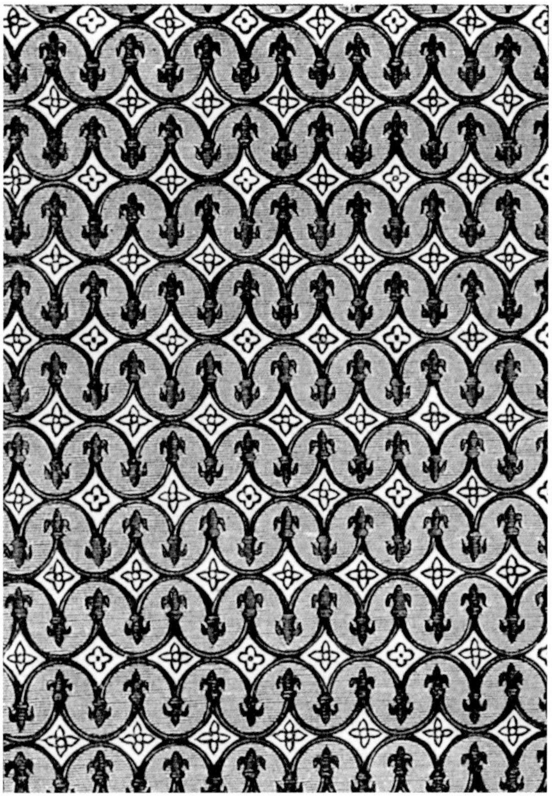

William Fry. Two contemporary images of furnishing fabrics from the *Art Journal*.

William Fry. Two contemporary images of furnishing fabrics from the *Illustrierte Katalog der Pariser Austellung*.

William Fry. Silk damask. PODR registered, June 1872.

William Fry. Furnishing fabric. PODR registered, December 1866.

William Fry. Silk. St Patrick's blue hanging. PODR registered, September 1871.

known to have recycled his designs and it is no surprise that he should have re-presented the design in a different medium.[22]

The reference to Arthur Silver (1853–1896) as a possible designer for 'Hera' was based on a report from Gordon Hunton in his book *English Decorative Textiles* claiming that the Rossendale Printing Company ran the design in 1870. At this time, Arthur Silver would have been 17 years old. In December 1876, Arthur Silver was employed by H. W. Batley, an eminent designer, and was to remain an employee with Batley for the rest of that decade.[23]

Hunton further claimed that Silver won a gold medal for the design of 'Hera' at the Manchester Exhibition 1877. No trace can be found of this exhibition but it may refer to the Jubilee Exhibition in 1887, where again no reference to 'Hera' can be identified. Moreover and importantly, there is no record of Fry's 'Hera' design in the Silver Studio archive.[24]

In 1975, on the occasion of the Liberty Centennial

William Fry. Silk damask. PODR registered, 1869.

William Fry. Silk damask. PODR registered, September 1871.

Exhibition at the V&A, the 'Hera' design was attributed to the Silver Studio on the basis of the Hunton report, which is the reason for the misattribution. In 2003, on first seeing the 1876 registration by Fry & Co., I discussed the attribution of 'Hera' with the curator of the Liberty exhibition, Barbara Morris. We discussed the new information in the light of Hunton and Morris very generously replied, 'I got it wrong.' We both agreed that the Hunton account was faulty.

Daniel Keith & Co., Spitalfields, London

Daniel Keith & Co. is known to have used designs by Pugin and Owen Jones. The company had a reputation for its fine work. Much interest was aroused by Keith's work for the Pasha of Egypt's new yacht in 1852. The company exhibited at the Great Exhibition. As for Norris & Co., some elements of the archives formerly held at Warner & Sons can no longer be traced but the former archivist noted that Dresser was recorded as having provided designs.[25]

William Fry. Bulrush design. PODR registered, April 1874.

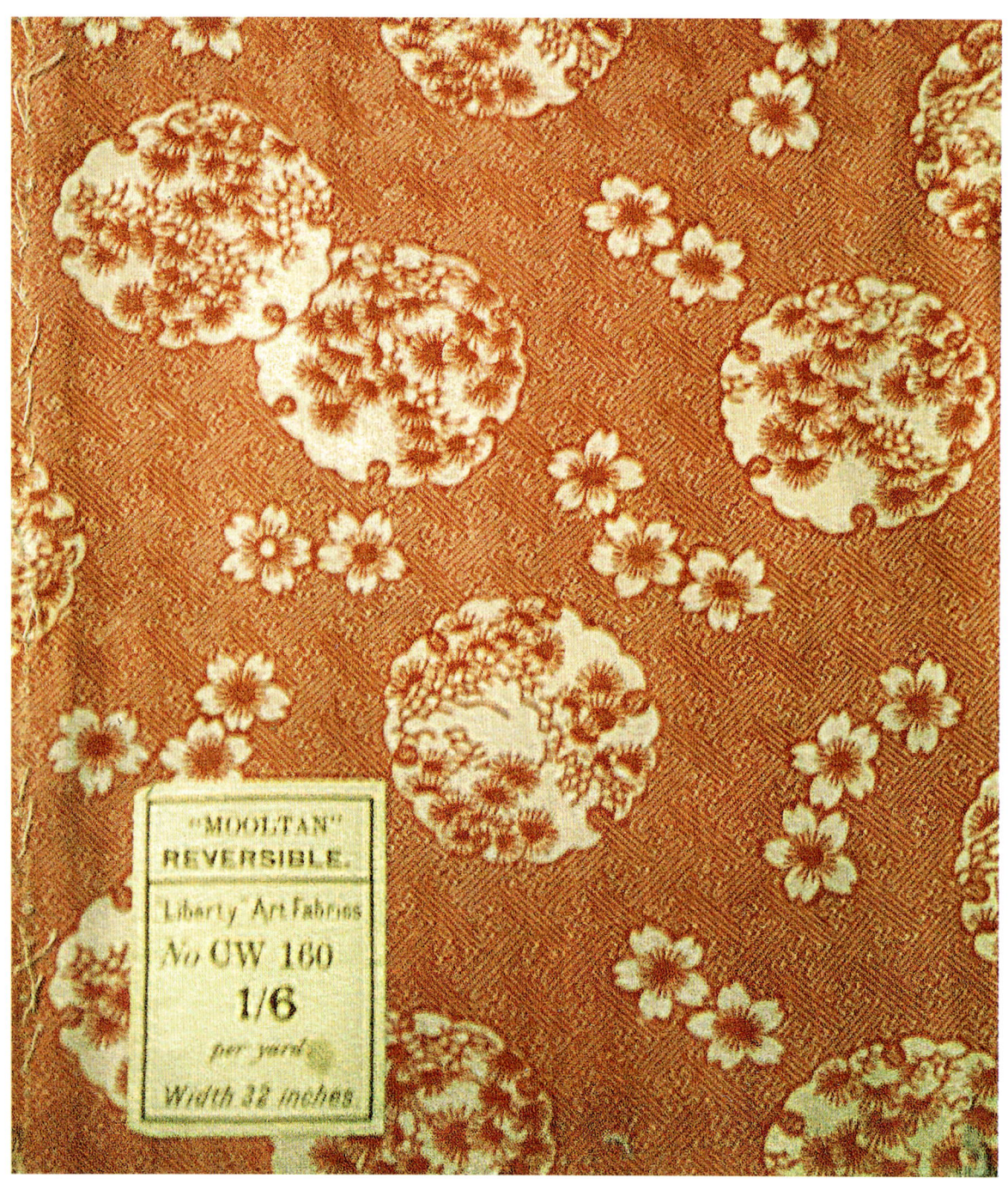

Liberty & Co., London

Liberty & Co. was founded in 1875 by Arthur Lasenby Liberty as the East India House—an oriental emporium. Arthur Liberty had previously worked in Regent Street with Farmers & Rogers, where he was in charge of the oriental department, but he quit on being refused a directorship and decided to open his own store. The new shop was successful and within a few years Liberty was able to expand its business. By 1885 with an extended frontage on Regent Street it was no longer exclusively an oriental emporium and had expanded into the main areas of the decorative arts with Liberty designing its own fabrics and furniture.

In 1881, Dresser claimed to be a 'designer for Liberty'.[26] Concurrently in 1881, Arthur Liberty became a shareholder in the Art Furnishers' Alliance in Bond Street, less than a kilometre distant. Liberty may have acted on the

Liberty. Design for silk. PODR registered, October 1880.

Opposite: Liberty. 'Mooltan' fabric. Label reads 'Mooltan reversible Liberty Art Fabrics No CW 160 1/6 [1s.6d] per yard. Width 32 inches'. (Courtesy of Liberty PLC)

The Lotus design was adopted by Liberty as a trademark for 'silk piece goods' in December 1886 and also featured on the mark for Clutha glass.

Liberty. Furnishing fabric. PODR registered, August 1884.

Liberty. Design for silk. PODR registered, June 1882.

schemes and assist customers to source items not held in stock and here the ability of Liberty to supply oriental items may have been the 'trigger' for Liberty's involvement. In this regard, it should be noted that Burroughs & Wellcome engaged the AFA to create a decorative scheme in the Anglo-Moorish style in 1882, which was completed in 1885.[27] These dates fit in with the launch of Liberty's own Anglo-Moorish range, and somewhat later, Liberty's advertisements offering to prepare decorative schemes for customers. Coincidentally, the Liberty Studio was established at the same time as the AFA ceased trading. By the 1890s Liberty & Co. was an internationally regarded name across the field of decorative arts and clothing.

The demise of the AFA in 1883 left Arthur Liberty (and Dresser) free to take advantage of a 'gap in the market'. It seems that Liberty & Co. was available to take over the supply of stock designed for the AFA. One such example is the chair on the left of the Liberty sketch as

encouragement of Dresser. Whatever the reason, Liberty's investment in his near neighbour, the AFA, requires an explanation.

A stated aim of the AFA was to discuss decorative

Liberty. Silk. PODR registered, April 1889.

Liberty. PODR registered, June 1904. (Courtesy of the National Archives)

Chair (left) designed by Dresser for manufacture by Thomas Knight, Bath and sold by Liberty as part of their Anglo-Moorish range.[28]

illustrated above. This chair was manufactured by the furniture-maker, Thomas Knight, Bath.[29] Knight was a creditor of the AFA in 1883. To this extent, I believe that Dresser and the AFA were a significant influence in the transition of Liberty & Co. from an oriental emporium into the general department store that we know today.

During the lifetime of Arthur Liberty, Liberty & Co. did not reveal the identity of designers. Dresser designed several items sold by Liberty, such as glass by James Coupar & Sons, Glasgow and painted galvanised tin chambersticks by R. Perry & Son, Wolverhampton, many of which carried a Dresser attribution, but this was for articles that Liberty bought directly from the manufacturer and were already inscribed with a Dresser 'signature'.

We know from the Dresser family tree that in 1881, Dresser regarded himself as a designer for Liberty.[30] Secondly, an article in the Liberty staff magazine reviewing the early days confirms that 'Dresser was an early business friend of the Head of our firm.'[31] Dresser could have materially helped Liberty through his knowledge of all things Japanese, including his own experience of visiting Japan and importing from the East.

Textile design was the first area of collaboration between Dresser and Liberty in the early 1880s. Designs were registered by Liberty at the PODR in the years 1880–1882 (see illustrations on pages 68, 69, 70, 71, 73). At this point in time, Dresser would have been creating designs in silk, at a time when Liberty Japanese silks were a major part of the Liberty brand and at a time before the Liberty Studio was established in 1883. Silks designed by Dresser may have been produced by George Holme of Derby, the family firm of Dresser's business partner, Charles Holme. There are numerous silks from this period in the Liberty archive carrying the marks 'GHD' for George Holme, Derby.

The direct connection between Liberty and Dresser had probably dwindled by the 1890s. By 1895, Liberty as a business operation was confident, forward-looking and expanding and had set up its own studio. It is somehow difficult to escape the suspicion that Liberty considered Dresser to be rather dated—as, indeed, was the entire Aesthetic movement by this time.

The Dresser style of ornament, though extensive, had developed from the floral forms of Gothic, the catholic styles of Owen Jones through the Japanese styles of the Aesthetic movement and the myriad international styles used in the textile industry. Dresser's designs for shape and form, still ground-breaking as with Perry, Old Hall, Clutha and Ault, were still recognisably Dresser. There was, however, a mood for something 'really new' even outrageous—akin, perhaps, to the Britain of the 1960s. The challenge for an entrepreneur like Arthur Lasenby Liberty was to see ahead and predict new trends, rather than merely react to them. By the 1890s, Morris, Crane and Day were already established favourites with the middle classes, while the styles of Voysey, Macintosh, Beardsley were new, in the ascendant and attracting the younger and more adventurous. Dresser also had a serious rival

Liberty. Design for cotton print registered in January 1882 as a printed fabric.

Liberty. Design registered as a printed fabric. PODR registered, October 1880.

Silk weave by Dresser for Norris & Co., 1870. Identified by Sue Kerry when archivist at Warner & Son Fabrics. (Courtesy of the Dorman Museum. Image by Jason Hynes)

in the Silver Studio, whose designs were sold by Liberty. Certainly, by the 1890s, Liberty had changed its image from being an oriental emporium into a progressive leader of style. Liberty's dwindling commitment to Dresser may have been the spur for Dresser to adapt his style. Charles Holme and Pevsner both refer to a change of style around this time; it is very noticeable. That he was able to adapt to the changing tastes and influences, both from his clients and from his young studio, is a sign of Dresser's strength as a designer. Many of the designs that came after 1895 were unlikely to be found in Dresser's personal archive. Nevertheless, the designs only left the studio after Dresser had vetted them and declared that they were technically feasible for the machines that would be manufacturing them. Even after Dresser stopped designing for Liberty, a family connection remained, as, in 1896, Dresser's son Louis Leo, joined the staff of 'B' Department in textiles. Louis Leo's association with Liberty has sometimes been romanticised as a design link—he was, in fact, a salesman in the shop. Prior to his employment at Liberty, Louis Leo was recorded in the 1891 census as a builder living in lodgings at 53, Kensington Church Street.

Norris & Co., London

Norris & Co. was established in the City of London in the eighteenth century. An advertisement in 1872 shows Norris to be a wholesale business supplying furniture silks, curtain borders, reps and velvets. The firm's archives were in the possession of Warner & Sons in 2004, but not all elements of that archive holding can be located. Before this time the archivist, Ms Sue Kerry, had noted that Dresser had designed for the firm, including the silk above.

Stead McAlpin, Carlisle

Stead McAlpin was founded in 1835 and, in the same year, an outlet was acquired in London. The company exhibited at the Society of Arts in 1848, winning a silver medal, followed by appearances at the 1851 and 1862 London exhibitions. The company was sold in 1965 and still exists today as part of the John Lewis Partnership.

The details of Dresser's work for Stead McAlpin are not recorded, though it is recorded that in 1878 the company printed some Dresser designs, which were later exhibited at Paris by another company, Barlow & Jones. It is also noteworthy that, during Dresser's time with Barlow & Jones, centres for quilts were bought in from Stead McAlpin.

The Stead McAlpin archive holds examples of nineteenth-century patterns which can be linked to Dresser through style and colour.

Stead McAlpin, 1878. Pattern 5807, border for hanging. (Courtesy of Stead McAlpin)

Stead McAlpin, c.1878. Pattern book with pattern numbers. (Courtesy of Stead McAlpin)

Stead McAlpin. PODR registered, November 1874. (Courtesy of the National Archives)

Stead McAlpin, 1878. Pattern 5712, border for hanging. (Courtesy of Stead McAlpin)

Stead McAlpin, 1878. Pattern 5783, filling for hanging. (Courtesy of Stead McAlpin)

Stead McAlpin, 1874. Pattern 5714, border for hanging. (Courtesy of Stead McAlpin)

Steinbach-Koechlin et Cie, Mulhouse

Steinbach Koechlin et Cie operated in Mulhouse, Alsace from 1852 until 1875. Mulhouse had a strong reputation for design generally, providing designs for manufacturers elsewhere in France and abroad. Indeed, even British cotton manufacturers, such as James Black and McNaughton & Thom, maintained design studios in Mulhouse. From the mid-1860s through to the early 1870s, Steinbach-Koechlin registered many designs with the British PODR; some were French in style, others were more English and showed a similarity to Dresser designs.

Remarks about Dresser designing for French companies and so reversing the trend of the French designing for British companies, were heard from several quarters in the 1860s. It is suggested that Steinbach-Koechlin is one such company Dresser provided with designs.

Above: Steinbach-Koechlin. Design for border. PODR registered, October 1867. (Courtesy of the National Archives)

Opposite: Steinbach-Koechlin. Design for filling. PODR registered, October 1866. (Courtesy of the National Archives)

Steinbach-Koechlin. Design for border. PODR registered, October 1867.

Steinbach-Koechlin. Design for border. PODR registered, November 1869. (Courtesy of the National Archives)

Steinbach-Koechlin. Design for border. PODR registered, November 1866. (Courtesy of the National Archives)

Steiner. Op art was alive in 1889. 'Op art' design for cotton print. PODR registered, September 1889. (Courtesy of the National Archives)

F. Steiner, Church, Accrington, Lancashire

In 1817, Frederick Steiner emigrated from Mulhouse to England, where he practised as a chemist developing dyes for turkey red printing. In 1836, Steiner acquired his own works near Accrington. Here he developed the turkey red processes, further reducing the manufacturing time. Though Frederick Steiner died in 1869, the business was carried on by his son and two daughters. Expansion became ever more rapid after 1880 and, in 1897, the company acquired limited liability. Though Dresser's connection with Steiner is well documented, details of his work, unfortunately, were not. However, according to Durant's interview with Frederick Burrows, Dresser had held a contract with Steiner. Both Charles Holme and Nikolaus Pevsner identified other Steiner/Dresser designs from the 'turn of the century'. The company closed in 1957, but not before it had contributed another design identified as 'Dresser', to the Cotton Board Exhibition of English chintz, 1957 (see page 94).

Steiner. Design for chintz. PODR registered, December 1902. (Courtesy of the National Archives)

Steiner. Design for chintz. PODR registered, October 1901.

Steiner. Design for chintz. PODR registered, December 1901. (Courtesy of the National Archives)

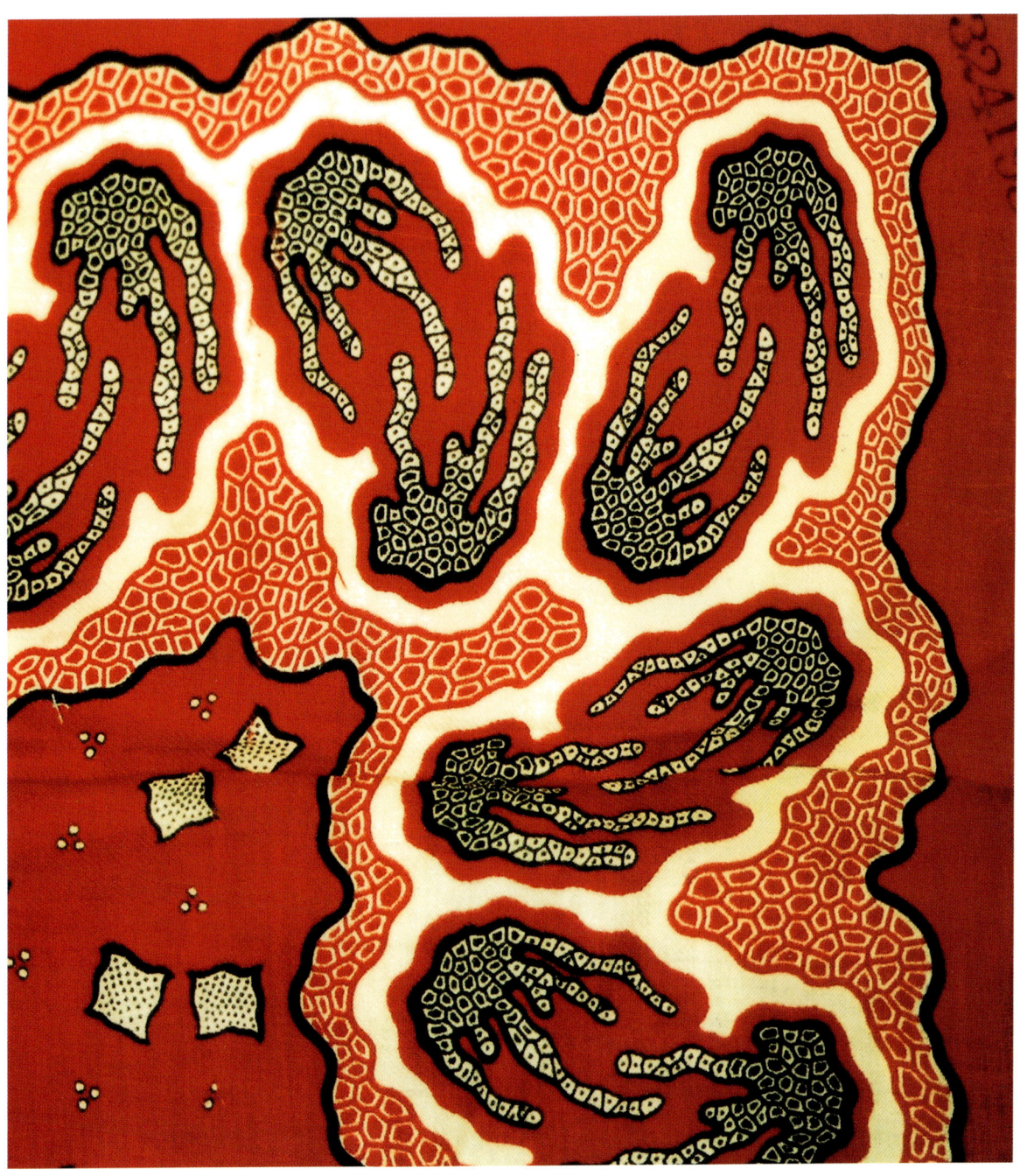

Steiner. Design for handkerchief. PODR registered, August 1898.

Steiner. Design for chintz. PODR registered, July 1902. (Courtesy of the National Archives)

Steiner. This design was noted by Pevsner. Design for heavy cotton print hanging. PODR registered, October 1896. Documented Dresser design. This textile is attached to a large original registration book and the weight of the book has resulted in creasing. (Courtesy of the National Archives)

Steiner. Design for handkerchief. Cotton print. PODR registered, March 1886. (Courtesy of the National Archives)

Opposite: Steiner. Cotton print design. (Courtesy of the National Archives)

F. Steiner. PODR registered, December 1896. (Courtesy of the National Archives)

F. Steiner. Design for window muslin, PODR registered, July 1890. (Courtesy of the National Archives)

F. Steiner. PODR registered, June 1890. (Courtesy of the National Archives)

Steiner. Design for chintz. PODR registered, December 1902. Pattern shown at the Cotton Board Exhibition, 1956, as 'Dresser'.

Opposite: Steiner. Design for chintz. PODR resitered, January 1898 (Courtesy of the National Archives)

Swaisland archive, Book 69. Furniture Colourings. c.1890. (Courtesy of G.P. & J. Baker)

Swaisland Fabric Printing Co., Crayford, Kent (Newman, Smith & Newman, Newgate Street, London)

Swaisland was well known to the London furnishing warehouses of the nineteenth century. Prominent among its customers was Newman, Smith & Newman. Swaisland was taken over in 1893, by G.P.&J. Baker, though the relationship continued until Newman, Smith & Newman started printing on its own account near Dartford. There is a design (with colour variations) in the Swaisland archive from a volume of patterns titled Furniture Colourings and annotated 'new Dresser' (opposite). Other designs (not annotated) in the Swaisland archive bear a stylistic similarity to Dresser designs; three of these are illustrated on this page. Dresser's links to Newman, Smith & Newman probably date from the 1870s, but the first documented evidence comes from the company being listed as one of the AFA's creditors. In 1899, Newman, Smith & Newman was referred to in the Studio[32] as owner of a Dresser cretonne design, which had previously been misattributed in the Dresser article of November 1898.

Swaisland. Three designs from the pattern books, bearing similarities to the Dresser style. Dated (from left to right) 1881, 1885, 1878 respectively. (Courtesy of G.P. & J. Baker)

Tootal Broadhurst, Lee, Manchester

Tootal Broadhurst, Lee gained international renown for the excellence of its weaves at the Paris Exhibition, 1878, winning the highest award—the Grand Prize. An American Government report at the time, considered Tootal to be a generation ahead of its competition. The two brothers, Henry and Joseph Lee, and Henry Tootal Broadhurst made up the senior members of the company and were responsible for its expansion and reputation. Henry Lee provided the organisational skills, Joseph the design and Henry Tootal Broadhurst the warehousing and sales skills. Tootal Broadhurst, Lee became a limited liability company in 1888.

The company had extensive international sales, including in Africa—an area that also inspired many of the intricate woven patterns. One design, a work plan for a woven article, possibly a quilt, is held in the Bolton Museum archive and carries the initials 'CD' (see opposite). Although the initials are not in Dresser's

Tootal Broadhurst, Lee. Woven design on textured cotton. PODR registered, August 1883. (Courtesy of the National Archives)

handwriting, it may have been annotated by a staff draughtsman. In his writings, Pevsner confirmed that Dresser sold designs to Tootal Broadhurst, Lee; this design is quite plausibly one such Dresser design.

Tootal Broadhurst, Lee. Print on textured cotton. PODR registered, August 1878. (Courtesy of the National Archives)

Opposite: Tootal Broadhurst, Lee, c.1880. Working design for woven cotton. Close-up shows initials 'CD' from lower left-hand corner. (Courtesy of Bolton Museum)

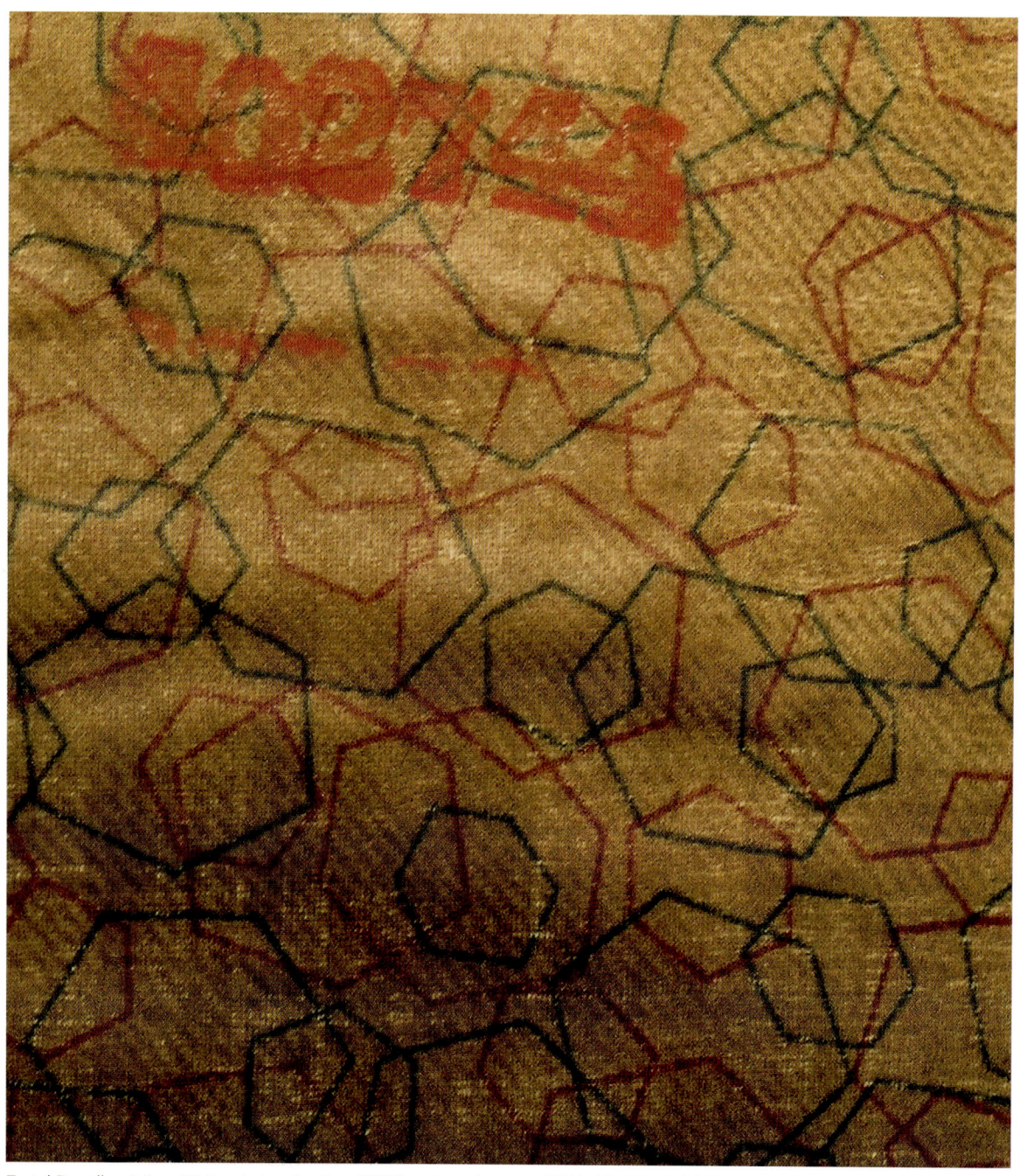
Tootal Broadhurst, Lee. Print on textured cotton. PODR registered, August 1883. (Courtesy of the National Archives)

Tootal Broadhurst, Lee. Woven design. PODR registered, September 1889. (Courtesy of the National Archives)

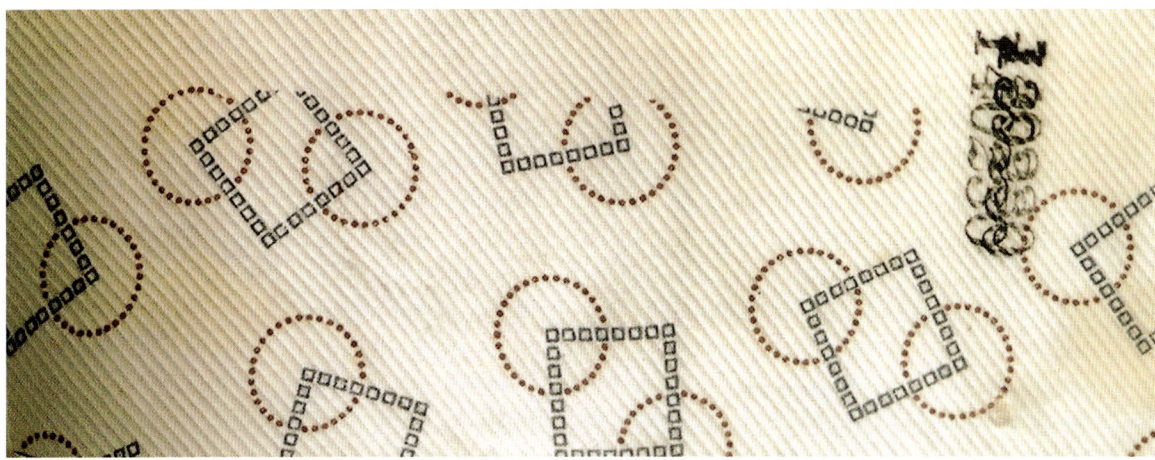

Tootal Broadhurst, Lee. Printed design on cotton. PODR registered, December 1889. (Courtesy of the National Archives)

Turnbull & Stockdale, Manchester

Turnbull & Stockdale was recorded by Pevsner as having manufactured Dresser's designs. No documented examples have been identified. However, many designs registered at the PODR bear similarities to the 'Dresser' style (see below). Later examples are in the art nouveau style for chintz.

Turnbull & Stockdale. Cotton print. PODR registered, March 1888. (Courtesy of the National Archives)

Turnbull & Stockdale. Cotton print. This sample is affixed to a page in a heavy book. (Courtesy of the National Archives)

J.W. & C. Ward, Halifax

J.W. & C. Ward was established in the early nineteenth century. Records show that Dresser designed the dining room interior decoration for the Halifax home of J.W. Ward in 1865. In 1871, the *Art Journal* illustrated four textiles shown at the London Exhibition that had been designed by Dresser for Ward.

Dresser was Art Advisor to Ward and the firm gained praise for its display at the London International Exhibition, 1871. The 1865 connection, together with an examination of Ward's registrations at the PODR from 1867 through to around 1875, gives this a measure of credibility. Also, interestingly, some of the drawings of furnishing textiles for PODR registrations by William Fry are in the same numbering series and style as those of Ward, pointing to a link between Fry and Ward in the mid-1870s.

Dresser had a marked influence on Ward's production, generating an increasing sophistication in design through the 1870s.

J.W. & C. Ward. Silk on wool furnishing fabric. Exhibited at the London International Exhibition, 1871.

J.W. & C. Ward. PODR registered, July 1871. This silk and wool furnishing textile was exhibited at the London International Exhibition, 1871.

J.W. & C. Ward. Silk on wool hanging. PODR registered, October 1873.

J.W. & C. Ward. Heavy silk and wool hanging. PODR registered, February 1868.

J.W. & C. Ward. Heavy silk and wool hanging. PODR registered, February 1868.

J.W. & C. Ward. Heavy silk and wool hanging. PODR registered, February 1868.

J.W. & C. Ward. Heavy silk and wool hanging. PODR registered, July 1872.

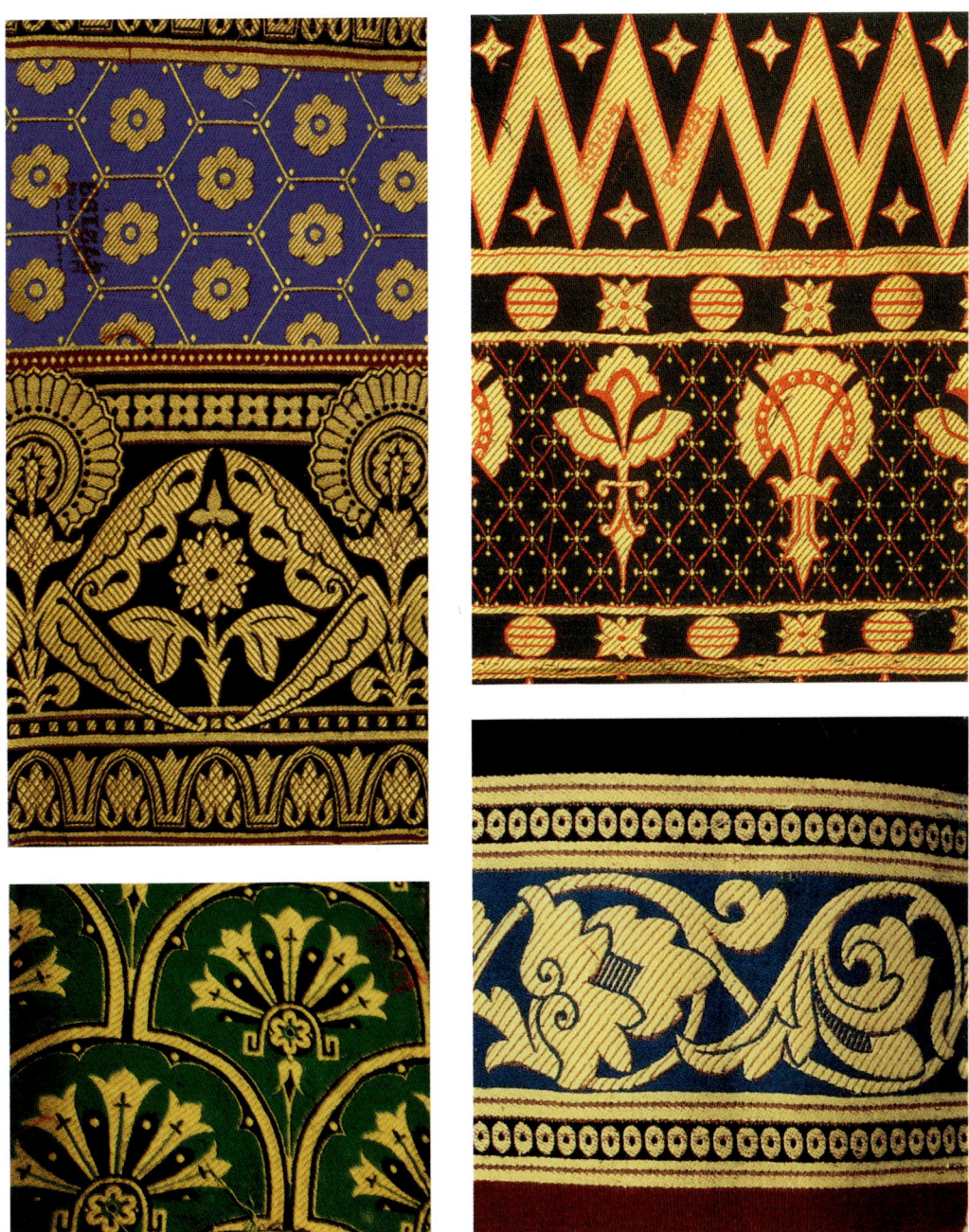

J.W. & C. Ward. Silk and wool hangings and one border. PODR registered, April 1872–October 1873.

J.W. & C. Ward. Silk and wool hangings. PODR registered, 1872. (Courtesy of the National Archives)

J.W. & C. Ward. Borders for hangings. Woven silk and wool. PODR registered, November 1872. (Courtesy of the National Archives)

J. Wilson, New Bond Street, London

John Wilson was a long-established linen draper at 159, New Bond Street by the time the Art Furnishers' Alliance purchased the lease of No.157 in 1880. The *Art Journal* published a linen damask by Dresser for Wilson (see right). Although Wilson regularly included Dresser's name in its list of designers as late as 1910, this is the only design that the company confirmed as being by Dresser. Wilson commissioned their designs for linen damask from Ireland Bros., Belfast.

John Wilson. Design for linen damask. Illustrated in the *Art Journal*, 1891, p.182.

This may be the only surviving example of a Dresser tablecloth. Detail of tablecloth by Dresser for John Wilson and manufactured by Ireland Bros., Belfast and Lurgan c.1891. Linen. Double damask. Length 366cm (12 feet), width 122cm (4 feet). Fleur de lys mark of Ireland Bros. (Courtesy of the Dorman Museum)

Textiles and Alsace

Alsace and its capital, Mulhouse, have been to France what Lancashire and Manchester have been to Britain since the eighteenth century when both countries learnt to print Indian designs on cotton. As the Musée de L'impression sur Etoffes, Mulhouse proclaims, 'The transformation of a woven design, created by an Indian craftsman into a printed motif onto cotton, wool or other fabrics is an example of consumer democracy. Textile printing enabled the more modest consumer to buy once unattainable items.'[33]

It is probable that Dresser sold designs to the Alsace textile manufacturers on a regular basis. Whereas I have not identified any Alsatian design with provenance, we know from members of Dresser's studio that he was 'doing business with every firm manufacturing wallpapers and cretonnes… When the Wallpaper Combine was formed[34] he went to Germany[35] and did extensive business with that country which he visited at intervals.'[36] Indeed, Dresser died during such a business trip in 1904. We also know that several Alsatian companies, such as Scheurer-Rott (later Scheurer Lauth), Koechlin and Dollfus Mieg, registered designs with the British Patent Office Design Registry, particularly in furnishing textiles.

Scheurer Rott, c.1884. Cotton furnishing fabric. (Courtesy of the Dorman Museum. Image by Jason Hynes)

Scheurer Lauth, c.1890. Cotton furnishing fabric. (Courtesy of the Dorman Museum. Image by Jason Hynes)

1. Durant's interview with Frederick Burrows, 1968.
2. Cecil Tattersall letter to the curator, Victorian and Edwardian Exhibition, 1952.
3. The Wallpaper Manufacturers Limited (WPM) was established in 1899 combining Britain's largest wallpaper manufacturers into one large combine.
4. Germany then included Alsace and Lorraine.
5. File note by Sir Caspar Purdon Clarke, Director of the V&A, in Dresser's file at the V&A, 1905.
6. Musee de l'Impression sur Etoffes de Mulhouse. These French companies sold in the UK.
7. *Cabinet Maker*, July 1892, p.17.
8. *Cabinet Maker*, July 1892, p.17.
9. The emphasis of Dresser's studio was now for flat conventional design. Frederick Burrows, an articled pupil for two years in the 1900s, was surprised to hear that Dresser had designed metalware. Interview with Stuart Durant and Frederick Burrows. Durant, Stuart (1993) *Christopher Dresser*. Ernst & Sohn, London, p.41.
10. Durant, Stuart (1993) *Christopher Dresser*. Ernst & Sohn, London, p.41.
11. Pevsner. Architectural Review, 1937, pp.183–6.
12. *Modern Ornamentation*, plate 3.
13. *Into Africa*. See catalogue for an exhibition at the Dorman Museum, 2007, illustration 032.
14. The Yoruba civilisation stretches across the southern coast of West Africa, crossing many countries from the Cameroons to Sierra Leone. The European powers divided up the land in the nineteenth century.
15. *Into Africa*. See catalogue for an exhibition by the Dorman Museum, Middlesbrough, 2007.
16. See *Modern Ornamentation*, plate 3.
17. Minutes of Evidence, para 740 from House of Commons report on The State of the Teaching of Art in Ireland, 1869.
18. The Silver Studio archive, The Museum of Domestic Design and Architecture (MODA), Middlesex University.
19. Minutes of Evidence, para 740 from House of Commons report on The State of the Teaching of Art in Ireland, 1869.
20. Ibid.
21. Aesthetic Movement Exhibition, V&A, 2011 credits 'Hera' to Arthur Silver (1853–1896), and at the time of writing (2017) the attribution to the Silver Studio appears on the V&A website.
22. Cotton print. For another example of Dresser's re-presentation of a design, see the 'fish' vase used by both Wedgwood and Linthorpe.
23. Henry William Batley (1846–1932) was highly regarded as a designer in the decorative arts, including schemes of decoration.
24. The Silver Studio archive, The Museum of Domestic Design and Architecture (MODA), Middlesex University.
25. Sue Kerry was archivist at Warners until c.2004.
26. Currently, there is no evidence of Liberty having a design staff before 1883, when Leonard Wyburd was appointed at the age of 18. See Bennett, Daryl (2012) *Liberty's Furniture*. Antique Collectors' Club, Woodbridge, p.89.
27. The Wellcome Trust archives, letter dated March 1885. Dresser is listed as a 'Designer for Liberty' on the Dresser family tree. Dorman Museum.
28. See the staff magazine, *Liberty Lamp*, May 1930, p.40.
29. Re: Thomas Knight, see Furniture Department, V&A archive.
30. The Dresser family tree. Dorman Museum. The Dresser family tree was regularly updated but the basic information that he was a 'designer for Liberty' is contemporary with the statement on the Dresser family tree that he was a designer for Linthorpe (1879–1881. The Dresser family tree also carries an endorsement that all information regarding (Dr) Christopher Dresser's family was provided by (Dr) Dresser himself.
31. *Liberty Lamp*, May 1930, p.40.
32. *The Studio*, Vol.XVI, March 1899.
33. http://www.musee-impression.com/gb/collection/xix.html
34. Leading British wallpaper companies merged into one co-operative in 1899.
35. Alsace was part of Germany between 1870 and 1918.
36. Durant–Burrows interview. Letter to the curator, Victorian and Edwardian Exhibition, 1952.

Victorian Design

The following are a selection of designs registered at the PODR by leading textile manufacturers and shipping agents in Britain in the latter part of the nineteenth century. No claim is being made here that any specific design is by Dresser, but the selection clearly shows the sophistication of design at that time. The examples should also dispel the image that the British textile industry was all mainstream 'Victorian'. These examples foreshadowed the forms of many a twentieth-century 'fine art' style and should equally dispel the myth that the decorative arts of the time were in any way reactive to the changing fancies of nineteenth and twentieth-century 'fine art'.

The illustrations represent the market that Dresser was selling into, especially in his last twenty years or so. Many of the companies can be identified as companies that Dresser worked with or sold designs to. Moreover, as Cecil Tattersall, a designer who worked for dresser for ten years (1894–1904), said:

'… You can take it that [Dresser] was doing business with every firm manufacturing wallpapers & cretonnes at that time …'

J.H. Calvert & Bros., Manchester. PODR registered, 1885.

Edwards, Cunliffe, Wilson, Glasgow. Origami birds. PODR registered, March 1881. (Courtesy of the National Archives)

Salis Schwabe, Manchester. PODR registered, November 1876.

J.H. Calvert & Bros., Manchester. PODR registered, 1885.

W.R. Graham & Co., Glasgow. PODR registered, October 1886.

McNaughton & Thom, Chorley (Manchester). PODR registered, 2 August 1883.

Fallows & Keymer, Manchester. PODR registered, September 1878. (Courtesy of the National Archives)

Tootal Broadhurst, Lee, Manchester. PODR registered, August 1883.

Henry Turner & Co., Manchester. Four designs, probably for clothing. PODR registered, November 1883. (Courtesy of the National Archives)

R. Dalglish Falconer. PODR registered, February 1893. (Courtesy of the National Archives)

R. Dalglish Falconer. PODR registered, July 1898. Echoes of the Festival of Britain motif. (Courtesy of the National Archives)

T.J. Birkin, Nottingham. Lace pattern PODR registered, October 1884. (Courtesy of the National Archives)

R. Dalglish Falconer, Glasgow. Three designs. PODR registered, March 1891. (Courtesy of the National Archives)

F.W. Grafton, Manchester. PODR registered, May 1892.

Herring, Hemmingway, Manchester. PODR registered, April 1892. (Courtesy of the National Archives)

Isaac, Bury, and Adelphi, Manchester. This small cutting in the National Archives may be of a sample for the export markets. PODR registered, December 1898. (Courtesy of the National Archives)

James Mills, Manchester. PODR registered, December 1902. (Courtesy of the National Archives)

Kinder Printing Co., Manchester. Although this design looks like an electric cardiograph, it was often the case that designs were influenced by scraps laying on the worktop. PODR registered, April 1881. (Courtesy of the National Archives)

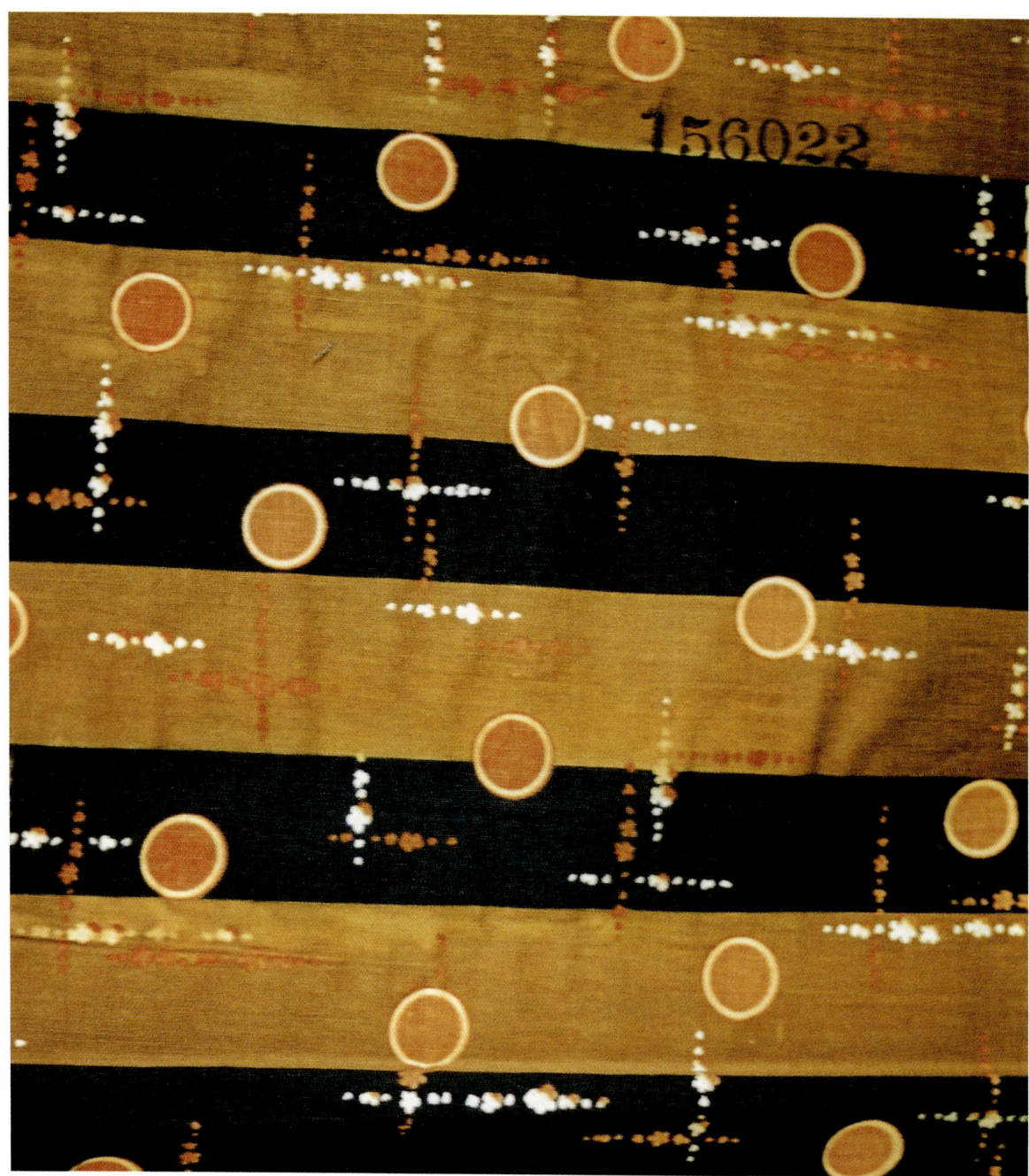

Inglis & Wakefield, Glasgow. PODR registered, September 1890. (Courtesy of the National Archives)

125

Stead McAlpin, Carlisle. PODR registered, October 1864. (Courtesy of the National Archives)

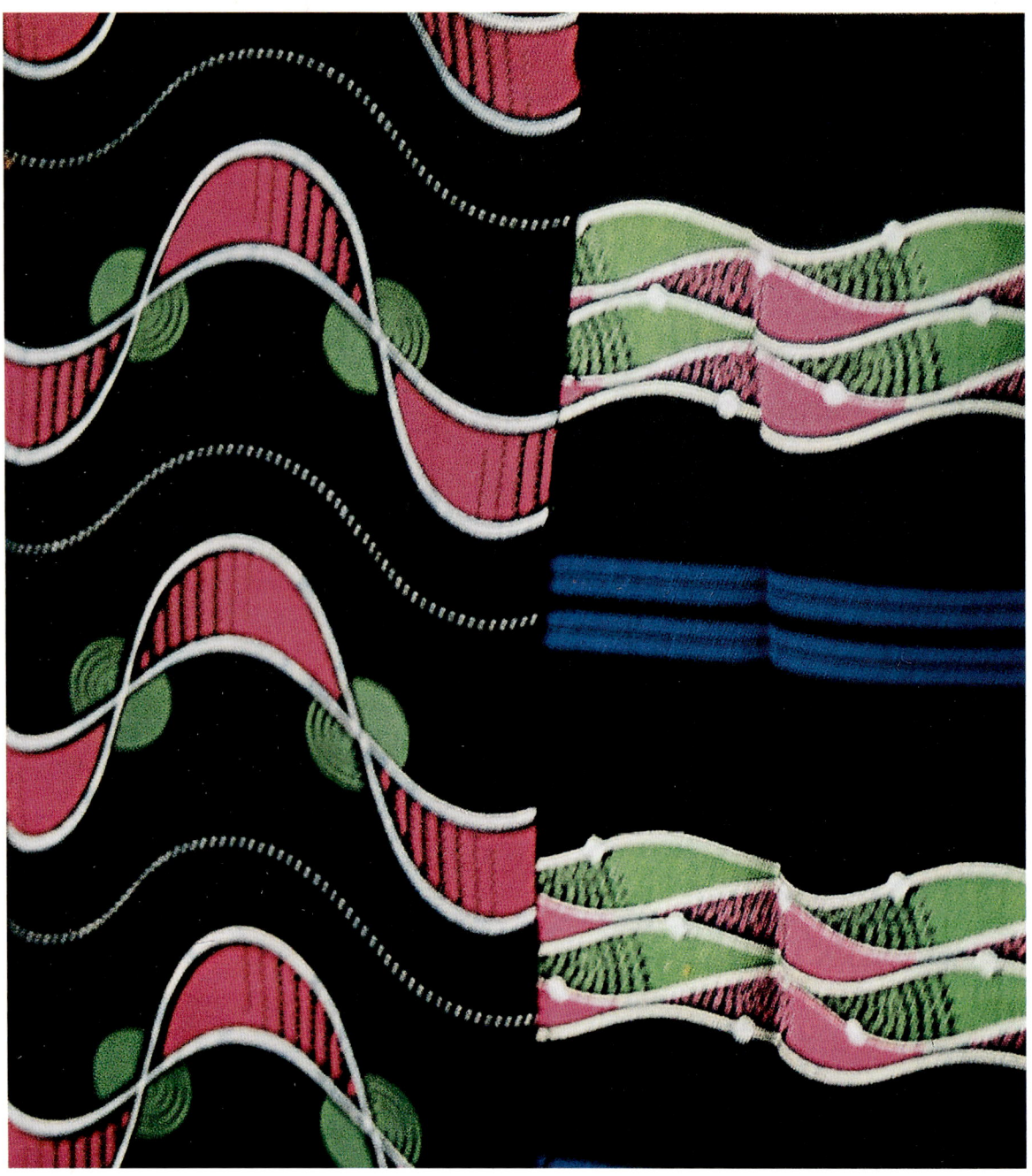
Two designs by Steiner registered in June 1904. Abstraction in furnishing fabrics was well developed by 1904.

Index

Page numbers in **bold** type refer to illustrations and captions

Aesthetic movement 7, 28, 30, 32, 33, 72
AFA see Art Furnishers' Alliance
African designs 52–59, **52–59**
Alexandra Palace Exhibition see under Exhibitions
Alsace 29, 38, 40, 81, 111
Art of Decorative Design, The 14, 16
Art Furnishers' Alliance 7, 26, 28, 32, 33, 48, 50, 69, 70, 72, 110
Art Journal, The 13, 14, 104, 110, **110**

Barlow & Jones 42, 43, 46, **46**, **47**, 75
Barlow, James see Barlow & Jones
Buckley, Ed & Jos 48, **48**, **49**
Burrows, Frederick 8, 9, 30, 38, 43, 52, 58, 85

Chicago Exhibition see under Exhibitions
Chromolithograph, The 20
Clarke, Caspar 14, 40
Clarkson, Thomas 40, 42, 50, **50**, **51**, 60
Coalbrookdale Co. 14
Creation Series, The 29, **39**, 52–59, **52–59**

Daniel Keith & Co. 66
Decorative art 20, 34, 35
Design reform 6, 7, 9, 26, 28
Doctorate from University of Jena 6, 13
Dresser family 12, 26, 28, 30, 72, 74
    Ada Rosa Nettleton (daughter) 8, 52
    Christopher (father) 12
    Christopher (son) 22
    Louis Leo (son) 30
Dresser signature 22, 70
Dresser Studio 8, **21**, 28–30, 38, 42
Dresser style 40, 42, 44
Dresser & Holme 8, 22, 23, 43, 44, 72, 74, 85
Dublin Exhibition see under Exhibitions

Edwards, Cunliffe, Wilson 39, **39**, 52–59, **52–59**, **114**
Exhibitions
    Chicago (1893) 46
    Dublin (1865) 60
    London (1851) 11, 14, 17, 66
    London (1862) 12, 13, 14, 16, 17, 35, 38, 40, 66
    London (1871) 40
    London (1872) 40
    London, Alexandra Palace (1873) 20, 22, 23, 32, 33, **33**
    Manchester (1887) 46
    Paris (1867) 20, 46, 62
    Paris (1878) 26, 46, 75, 99
    Vienna (1873) 32

Falconer, R. Dalglish **119**, **120**
Fine Art Society 8
Flat decoration 42
Furniture Gazette 22, 23, 28
Fry, William & Co. 40, 42, 43, 50, **50**, 60–66, **60–66**

Godwin, Edward W. 9
Great Exhibition, London see under Exhibitions

Hera design 60, **60**, **61**, 62, 65, 66
Holme & Co. see Dresser & Holme
Holme, Charles see Dresser & Holme

'Ipswich' sketch book 16, 57, **57**

Japan
    Exhibitions 8
    Influence on Dresser's work 23, 72
    Visit 22, 72
Jena, University 6, 13
Jones, Owen 6, 13, **13**, 16, 35, 40, 42, 66, 72
Jones, Thomas see Barlow & Jones

Kemp, Clisby 7

Liberty, Arthur Lasenby see Liberty & Co.
Liberty & Co. 26, 29, 33, 42, 43, 60, **60**, **61**, 65, 66, 69–74, **69–74**
Linnean Society 26
Linthorpe 7, 22, 23, 26, 34
London Exhibitions see under Exhibitions

Manchester Exhibition see under Exhibitions
Minton & Co. 12, 14, **15**, 34
Morris, Barbara 66
Morris, William 7, 11, 14, 44, 50, 72

Norris & Co. 74, **74**

Paris Exhibitions see under Exhibitions
Perry, Richard & Son 28, 29, 72
Pevsner, Sir Nikolaus 8, 42–44, 52, 74, 85, 99, 102

Royal Society of Arts 20
Ruskin, John 14, 16

Scheurer Rott see Scheurer Lauth
Scheurer Lauth **18–19**, **24–25**, 40, 111, **111**, 112
School of Design, London 6, 11–14, 16, 32, 35, 38
Silver, Arthur see Silver Studio
Silver Studio 44, 60, 62, 65, 66, 72
Stead McAlpin 42, 50, 75, **75**, **76–79**, 125
Steinbach-Koechlin et Cie **31**, 81, **80**, **81–83**
Steiner, F. & Co. 29, 42, **43**, **44–45**, 54, 56, 85, **84–126**
Studio, The 8, 22
Swaisland Printing Co. 42, **96**, 97, **97**

Tattersall, Cecil 38, 42, 114
Tootal Broadhurst, Lee 40, 42, 43, 99, **98–101**, **118**
Turnbull & Stockdale 43, 102, **102**, **103**

Vienna Exhibition see under Exhibitions

Wallis, George 6, 7, 35
Ward, James & Co. 40, **41**, 42, 104, **104–109**
Warner & Sons 66, 74, **74**
Wilson, John & Sons **36–37**, 110, **110**

About the Author

Harry Lyons's passion for Christopher Dresser goes back many years: he has searched out a huge range of previously unrecognised Dresser designs. Harry has frequently lectured and written on Dresser, and held a ground-breaking exhibition of the designer's work at the New Century Gallery in 1999. He was also a major contributor to the Cooper Hewitt 2004 Dresser exhibition catalogue, in New York and at the V&A, London.

Acknowledgements

My thanks to Gill Moore and the staff of the Dorman Museum, Middlesbrough, Peter Andow, Daryl Bennett, Sue Bennett, Alastair Carew-Cox, Andrew Everett, Sue Kerry, Patrick McIntosh Patrick, John Scott, David Taylor and Michael Whiteway for their encouragement and help, and for the use of photographs.

To see the full catalogue of books published by ACC Art Books, please go to our website:
www.accartbooks.com

ACC Art Books
Sandy Lane, Old Martlesham,
Woodbridge, Suffolk, IP12 4SD, UK
Tel: 01394 389950
email: uksales@accpublishinggroup.com

ACC Distribution
6 West 18th Street, Suite 4B
New York NY10011, USA
Tel: 212 645 1111
email: ussales@accpublishinggroup.com